THE WISDOM OF ISRAEL REGARDIE

◎ ◎ ◎ ◎ ◎

VOLUME I
SELECTED INTRODUCTIONS, PREFACES AND FOREWORDS

INTRODUCTION BY
LON MILO DUQUETTE

Some Other Titles From New Falcon Publications

Aha! The Sevenfold Mystery of the Ineffable Love — **Aleister Crowley**
Bio-Etheric Healing — **Trudy Lanitis**
Undoing Yourself With Energized Meditation and Other Devices
Secrets of Western Tantra: The Sexuality of the Middle Path
Dogma Daze — **Christopher S. Hyatt, Ph.D.**
Rebels & Devils; The Psychology of Liberation **Edited by Christopher S. Hyatt, Ph.D.**
Aleister Crowley's Illustrated Goetia
Taboo: Sex, Religion & Magick
Sex Magic, Tantra & Tarot: The Way of the Secret Lover
    Christopher S. Hyatt, Ph.D., and Lon Milo DuQuette
Pacts With The Devil
Urban Voodoo: A Beginner's Guide to Afro-Caribbean Magic
    Jason Black and Christopher S. Hyatt, Ph.D.
The Psychopath's Bible — **Christopher S. Hyatt, Ph.D., and Jack Willis**
Ask Baba Lon — **Lon Milo DuQuette**
Aleister Crowley and the Treasure House of Images **J.F.C. Fuller, Aleister Crowley,**
    Lon Milo DuQuette and Nancy Wasserman
Enochian World of Aleister Crowley **Lon Milo DuQuette and Aleister Crowley**

Info-Psychology   Neuropolitique   The Game of Life
What Does WoMan Want? — **Timothy Leary, Ph.D.**

Be Yourself - A Guide to Relaxation and Health
Dr. Israel Regardie's Definitive Work on Aleister Crowley, The Eye In The Triangle
Healing Energy, Prayer and Relaxation
My Rosicrucian Adventure
Teachers of Fulfillment
The Complete Golden Dawn System of Magic
The Eye in the Triangle: An Interpretation of Aleister Crowley
The Golden Dawn Audio CDs
The Legend of Aleister Crowley
The Portable Complete Golden Dawn System of Magic
The Tree of Life
What You Should Know About the Golden Dawn — **Dr. Israel Regardie**

Roll Away The Stone/The Herb Dangerous — **Dr. Israel Regardie and Aleister Crowley**

Rebellion, Revolution and Religiousness — **Osho**
Reichian Therapy: A Practical Guide for Home Use — **Dr. Jack Willis**
Woman's Orgasm: A Guide to Sexual Satisfaction — **Benjamin Graber, M.D.,**
    and Georgia Kline-Graber, R.N.
Shaping Formless Fire   Seizing Power   Taking Power — **Stephen Mace**
The Illuminati Conspiracy: The Sapiens System — **Donald Holmes, M.D.**
The Secret Inner Order Rituals of the Golden Dawn — **Pat Zalewski**
Sufism, Islam and Jungian Psychology — **J. Marvin Spiegelman, Ph.D.**
Nonlocal Nature: The Eight Circuits of Consciousness — **James A. Heffernan**
on What is — **Ja Wallin**

MANY OF OUR TITLES AVAILABLE ON KINDLE!
Please visit our website at http://www.newfalcon.com

THE WISDOM OF
ISRAEL REGARDIE

೦∕೦ ೦∕೦ ೦∕೦ ೦∕೦ ೦∕೦

Volume I
SELECTED INTRODUCTIONS, PREFACES AND FOREWORDS

Introduction by
Lon Milo DuQuette

NEW FALCON PUBLICATIONS
LAS VEGAS, NEVADA, U.S.A.

Copyright © 2018 New Falcon Publications

All rights reserved. No part of this book,
in part or in whole, may be reproduced, transmitted,
or utilized, in any form or by any means, electronic or mechanical,
including photocopying, recording, or by any information storage
and retrieval system, without permission in writing
from the publisher, except for brief quotations
in critical articles, books and reviews.

ISBN 13: 978-1-56184-547-7
ISBN 10: 1-56184-547-7

New Falcon Publications First Edition

The paper used in this publication meets the minimum requirements
of the American National Standard for Permanence of
Paper for Printed Library Materials Z39.48-1984

Printed in USA

NEW FALCON PUBLICATIONS
9550 South Eastern Avenue • Suite 253
Las Vegas, NV 89123
www.newfalcon.com
email: info@newfalcon.com

Introduction

Genius Can Be Infectious
By Lon Milo DuQuette

In my introductory words to the New Falcon Publications edition of *Dr. Israel Regardie's Definitive Work on Aleister Crowley - The Eye in the Triangle*[1] I confess:

> *"No matter what you may have read to the contrary on the internet, I was not Regardie's 'magical apprentice.' Nor was I his formal student. I was never personally 'initiated' by him into any kind of Golden Dawn, or A∴A∴ or O.T.O.,[2] or anything. I can, however, proudly (and with no small measure of awe and humility) claim him as one of my earliest and most influential magical mentors. He made himself available whenever I had specific questions about magick and Crowley, and he was generous with his time, information and opinions. He was also supportive of our O.T.O. Lodge[3] in Newport Beach, and donated duplicate books from his own substantial library, and other magical trinkets."*

---

[1] *Dr. Israel Regardie's Definitive Work on Aleister Crowley-The Eye in the Triangle*, New Falcon Publishing, First Edition 2017.

[2] We *were* both members of the Masonic youth organization, the Order of DeMolay, and upon discovery of this fact both stood up, and exchanged the Sign, Grip, and Secret Word of a DeMolay initiate.

[3] Heru-ra-ha Lodge Ordo Templi Orientis, chartered Jan.7th, 1978 by Hymenaeus Alpha 777 (Grady L. McMurtry). H.R.H. Lodge is the first local O.T.O. Lodge chartered under the auspices of the Grand Lodge of the United States, and remains the oldest continuously operating O.T.O. body in the world.

Regardie initially gained the attention and admiration of the esoteric and occult community by his 1931 qabalistic primer, *A Garden of Pomegranates* which was almost immediately followed in 1932 by *The Tree of Life*. Both works are brilliant and deserving of occult immortality, but would soon be overshadowed by his controversial decision to publish (1937-1940) much of the (until then) "secret" magical teachings of the Hermetic *Order of the Golden Dawn* and its subsequent organizational incarnation, the *Stella Matutina*.

His credentials to write with insight and authority on such esoteric and arcane subjects were deservedly earned by his own scholarship, intelligence and brilliance, but his 'apprenticeship' (1928-1932) to Aleister Crowley would remain perhaps the most important item on his resume. If genius can said to be infectious it is easy to observe how it spread from Crowley to Regardie, and there is no question that their brief association knocked decades off young Regardie's learning curve. But I believe it also did something else.

Regardie lived and worked with Crowley during one of the most important and pivotal phases of Crowley's spiritual growth and development. Yes, Regardie was learning technical aspects of magick and esoteric philosophy, but more importantly he was experiencing firsthand the character-building effects (both positive and negative) that the illumination of a master has upon a student.

The two would eventually have a well-publicized falling-out, and Regardie would go on to make an honored and respectable name for himself. But, for better or worse, he would always remain somewhat in the shadow of the Great Beast, and in my opinion that is not necessarily a bad thing. I believe that because it is clear to me that to some degree *genius is infectious*.

I, for one, feel blessed to have had the opportunity to rub elbows with the genius of Israel Regardie, and am thrilled that his works, large and small are being made available to new generations.

Table of Contents

Introduction by *Lon Milo DuQuette* v

Introductions

A Garden of Pomegranates 3
The Tree of Life, A Study in Magic 13
Dr. Israel Regardie's Definitive Work on Aleister Crowley
  The Eye In the Triangle 17
The Philosopher's Stone 27
The Legend of Aleister Crowley 35
Dr. Christopher S. Hyatt's *Undoing Yourself* 51
Roll Away the Stone 53
My Rosicrucian Adventure 113
Aleister Crowley's *The Law is For All* 121
Robert Anton Wilson's *Prometheus Rising* 143
The Complete Golden Dawn System of Magic 149

Prefaces

Aleister Crowley's *Gems From The Equinox* 173
Healing Energy, Prayer and Relaxation 195
Aleister Crowley's *The Holy Books* 197

Forewords

The Middle Pillar 201
Edwin C. Steinbrecher's *The Inner Guide Meditation* 227
The Teachers of Fulfillment 229

INTRODUCTIONS
by Israel Regardie

A GARDEN OF POMEGRANATES
New Falcon Publications, First Edition, 2018

It is ironic that a period of the most tremendous technological advancement known to recorded history should also be labeled the Age of Anxiety. Reams have been written about modern man's frenzied search for his soul—and, indeed, his doubt that he even has one at a time when, like castles built on sand, so many of his cherished theories, long mistaken for verities, are crumbling about his bewildered brain.

The age-old advice, "Know thyself," is more imperative than ever. The tempo of science has accelerated to such a degree that today's discoveries frequently make yesterday's equations obsolescent almost before they can be chalked up on a blackboard. Small wonder, then, that every other hospital bed is occupied by a mental patient. Man was not constructed to spend his life at a crossroads, one of which leads he knows not where, and the other to threatened annihilation of his species.

In view of this situation it is doubly reassuring to know that even in the midst of chaotic concepts and conditions there still remains a door through which man, individually, can enter into a vast store house of knowledge, knowledge as dependable and immutable as the measured tread of Eternity.

For this reason, I am especially pleased to be writing an introduction to a new edition of *A Garden of Pomegranates*. I feel that never, perhaps, was the need more urgent for just such a road map as the Qabalistic system provides. It should be equally useful to any who choose to follow it, whether he be Jew, Christian, Buddhist, Deist, Theosophist, agnostic or atheist.

The Qabalah is a trustworthy guide, leading to a comprehension both of the Universe and one's own Self. Sages have long taught that Man is a miniature of the Universe, containing within himself the diverse elements of that macrocosm. Within the Qabalah is a glyph called the Tree of Life which is at once a symbolic map of the Universe in its major aspects, and also of its smaller counterpart, Man.

Manly P. Hall, in *The Secret Teachings of All Ages*, deplores the failure of modern science to "sense the profundity of these philosophical deductions of the ancients." Were they to do so, he says, they "would realize those who fabricated the structure of the Qabalah possessed a knowledge of the celestial plan comparable in every respect with that of the modern savant."

Fortunately, many scientists in the field of psychotherapy are beginning to sense this correlation. In Francis G. Wickes' *The Inner World of Choice* reference is made to "the existence in every person of a galaxy of potentialities for growth marked by a succession of personalogical evolution and interaction with environments." She points out that man is not only an individual particle but "also a part of the human stream, governed by a Self greater than his own individual self."

The Book of the Law states simply, "Every man and every woman is a star." This is a startling thought for those who considered a star a heavenly body, but a declaration subject to proof by anyone who will venture into the realm of his own Unconscious. This realm, he will learn if he persists, is not hemmed in by the boundaries of his physical body but is one with the boundless reaches of outer space.

Those who, armed with the tools provided by the Qabalah, have made the journey within and crossed beyond the barriers of illusion, have returned with an impressive quantity of knowledge which conforms strictly to the definition of "science" in Winston's College Dictionary: "Science: a body of knowledge, general truths of particular facts, obtained and shown to be correct by accurate observation and thinking; knowledge condensed, arranged and systematized with reference to general truths and laws."

Over and over their findings have been confirmed, proving the Qabalah contains within it not only the elements of the science itself but the method with which to pursue it.

When planning to visit a foreign country, the wise traveler will first familiarize himself with its language. In studying music, chemistry or calculus, a specific terminology is essential to the understanding of each subject. So a new set of symbols is necessary when undertaking a study of the Universe, whether within or without. The Qabalah provides such a set in unexcelled fashion.

But the Qabalah is more. It also lays the foundation on which rests another archaic sleight-of-hand, Magic has been defined by Aleister Crowley as "the science and art of causing change to occur in conformity with will." Dion Fortune qualifies this nicely with an added clause, "changes in consciousness."

The Qabalah reveals the nature of certain physical and psychological phenomena. Once these are apprehended, understood and correlated, the student can use the principles of Magic to exercise control over life's conditions and circumstances not otherwise possible. In short, Magic provides the practical application of the theories supplied by the Qabalah.

It serves yet another vital function. In addition to the advantages to be gained from its philosophical application, the ancients discovered a very practical use for the literal Qabalah.

Each letter of the Qabalistic alphabet has a number, color, many symbols and a Tarot card attributed to it. The Qabalah not only aids in an understanding of the Tarot, but teaches the student how to *classify* and organize all such ideas, numbers and symbols. Just as a knowledge of Latin will give insight into the meaning of an unfamiliar English word with a Latin root, so the knowledge of the Qabalah with the various attributions to each character in its alphabet will enable the students to understand and correlate ideas and concepts which otherwise would have no apparent relation.

A simple example is the concept of the Trinity in the Christian religion. The student is frequently amazed to learn through a study of the Qabalah that Egyptian mythology followed a similar concept with its trinity of gods, Osiris the father, Isis the virgin-mother, and Horus the son. The Qabalah indicated similar correspondences in the pantheon of Roman and Greek deities, proving the father-mother (Holy Spirit) - son principles of deity are primordial archetypes of man's psyche, rather than being, as is frequently and erroneously supposed, a development peculiar to the Christian era.

At this juncture let me call attention to one set of attributions by Rittangelius usually found as an appendix attached to the *Sepher Yetzirah*. It lists a series of "Intelligences" for each one of the ten Sephiros and the twenty-two Paths of the Tree of Life. It seems to me, after prolonged meditation, that the common attributions of these Intelligences is altogether arbitrary and lacking in serious meaning.

For example, *Keser* is called 'The Admirable or the Hidden Intelligence.' It is the Primal Glory, for no created being can attain to its essence." This seems perfectly all right; the meaning at first sight to fit the significance of *Keser* as the first emanation from *Ain Soph*. But there are half a dozen other similar attributions that would have served equally well. For instance, it could have been called the "Occult Intelligence" usually attributed to the seventh Path or *Sephirah*, for surely *Keser* is secret in a way to be said of no other *Sephirah*. And what about the "Absolute or Perfect Intelligence." That would have been even more explicit and appropriate, being applicable to *Keser* far more than to any other of the Paths. Similarly, there is one attributed to the 16th Path and called "The Eternal or Triumphant Intelligence," so-called because it is the pleasure of the Glory, beyond which is no Glory like to it is called also the Paradise prepared for the Righteous." Any of these several would have done equally well. Much is true of so many of the other attributions in this particular area–that is the so-called Intelligences of the *Sepher Yetzirah*. I do not think that their use or current arbitrary usage stands up to serious examination or criticism.

A good many attributions in other symbolic areas, I feel, are subject to the same criticism. The Egyptian Gods have been used with a good deal of carelessness, and without sufficient explanation of motives in assigning them as I did. In a recent edition of Crowley's masterpiece *Liber 777* (which *au fond* is less a reflection of Crowley's mind as a recent critic claimed than a tabulation of some of the material given piecemeal in the Golden Dawn knowledge lectures), he gives for the first time brief explanations of the motives for his attributions. I, too, should have been far more explicit in the explanations I used in the case of some of the Gods whose names were used many times, most inadequately, where several paths were concerned. While it is true that the religious coloring of the Egyptian Gods differed from time to time during Egypt's turbulent history, nonetheless, a word or two about just that one single point could have served a useful purpose.

Some of the passages in the book force me today to emphasize that so far as the Qabalah is concerned, it could and should be employed without binding to it the partisan qualities of any one particular religious faith. This goes as much for Judaism as it does for Christianity. Neither has much intrinsic usefulness where this scientific scheme is concerned. If some students feel hurt by this statement, that cannot be helped. The day of most contemporary faiths is over; they have been more of a curse than a boon to mankind. Nothing that I say here, however, should reflect on the peoples concerned, those who accept these religions. They are merely unfortunate. The religion itself is worn out and indeed is dying.

The Qabalah has nothing to do with any of them. Attempts on the part of cultish-partisans to impart higher mystical meanings through the Qabalah, etc., to their now sterile faiths is futile, and will be seen as such by the younger generation. They, the flower and love children, will have none of this nonsense.

I felt this a long time ago, as I still do, but even more so. The only way to explain the partisan Jewish attitude demonstrated in some small sections of the book can readily be explained. I had been reading some writings of Arthur Edward Waite, and some of his pomposity and turgidity stuck to my mantle. I disliked his patronising Christian attitude, and so swung all the way over to the other side of the pendulum. Actually, neither faith is particularly important in this day and age. I must be careful never to read Waite again before embarking upon literary work of my own.

Much knowledge obtained by the ancients through the use of the Qabalah has been supported by discoveries of modern scientists–anthropologists, astronomer, psychiatrists, *et al.* Learned Qabalists for hundreds of years have been aware of what the psychiatrist has only discovered in the last few decades–that man's concept of himself, his deities and the Universe is a constantly evolving process, changing as man himself evolves on a higher spiral. But the roots of his concepts are buried in a race-consciousness that antedated Neanderthal man by uncounted aeons of time. What Jung calls archetypal images constantly rise to the surface of man's awareness from the vast unconscious that is the common heritage of all mankind.

The tragedy of civilized man is that he is cut off from awareness of his own instincts. The Qabalah can help him achieve the necessary understanding to effect a reunion with them, so that rather than being driven by forces he does not understand, he can harness for his conscious use the same power that guides the homing pigeon, teaches the beaver to build a dam and keeps the planets revolving in their appointed orbits about the sun.

I began the study of the Qabalah at an early age. Two books I read then have played unconsciously a prominent part in the writing of my own book. One of these was "Q.B.L. or the Bride's Reception" by Frater Achad (Charles Stansfeld Jones) which I must have first read around 1926. The other was "An Introduction to the Tarot" by Paul Foster Case, published in early 1920. It is now out of print, superseded by later versions of the same topic. But, as I now glance through this slender book, I perceive how profoundly even the format of his book has influenced me, though in these two instances there was not a trace of plagiarism. It had not consciously occurred to me until recently that I owed so much to them. Since Paul Case passed away about a decade or so ago, this gives me the opportunity to thank him, overtly, wherever he may now be.

By the middle of 1926 I had become aware of the work of Aleister Crowley, for whom I have a tremendous respect. I studied as many of his writings as I could gain access to, making copious notes, and later acted for several years as his secretary, having joined him in Paris on October 12, 1928, a memorable day in my life.

All sorts of books have been written on the Qabalah, some poor, some few others extremely good. But I came to feel the need for what might be called a sort of Berlitz handbook, a concise but comprehensive introduction, studded with diagrams and tables of easily understood definitions and correspondences to simplify the student's grasp of so complicated and abstruse a subject.

During a short retirement in North Devon in 1931, I began to amalgamate my notes. It was out of these that *A Garden of Pomegranates* gradually emerged. I unashamedly admit that my book contains many direct plagiarisms from Crowley, Waite, Eliphas Levi, and D. H. Lawrence. I had incorporated numerous fragments from their works into my notebooks without citing individual references to the various sources from which I condensed my notes.

Prior to the closing down of the Mandrake Press in London about 1930-31, I was employed as company secretary for a while. Along with several Crowley books, the Mandrake Press published a lovely little monogram by D. H. Lawrence entitled "*Apropos of Lady Chatterley's Lover.*" My own copy accompanied me on my travels for long years. Only recently did I discover that it had been lost. I hope that any one of my former patients who had borrowed it will see fit to return it to me forthwith.

The last chapter of *A Garden* deals with the Way of Return. It used almost entirely Crowley's concept of the Path as described in his superb essay "One Star in Sight." In addition to this, I borrowed extensively from Lawrence's *Apropos*. Somehow, they all fitted together very nicely. In time, all these variegated notes were incorporated into the text without acknowledgment, an oversight which I now feel sure would be forgiven, since I was only twenty-four at the time.

Some modern Nature-worshippers and members of the newly-washed and redeemed witch-cult have complimented me on this closing chapter which I entitled "The Ladder." I am pleased about this. For a very long time I was not at all familiar with the topic of witchcraft. I had avoided it entirely, not being attracted to its literature in any way. In fact, I only became slightly conversant with its theme and literature just a few yeas ago, after reading "The Anatomy of Eve" written by Dr. Leopold Stein, a Jungian analyst. In the middle of his study of four cases, he included a most informative chapter on the subject. This served to stimulate me to wider reading in that area.

In 1932, at the suggestion of Thomas Burke, the novelist, I submitted my manuscript to one of his publishers, Messrs. Constable in London. They were unable to use it, but made some encouraging comments and advised me to submit to Riders. To my delight and surprise, Riders published it, and throughout the years the reaction it has had indicated other students found it also fulfilled their need for a condensed and simplified survey of such a vast subject as the Qabalah.

The importance of the book to me was and is five-fold: 1) it provided a yardstick by which to measure my personal progress in the understanding of the Qabalah; 2) therefore it can have an equivalent value to the modern student; 3) it serves as a theoretical introduction to the Qabalistic foundation of the magical work of the Hermetic Order of the Golden Dawn; 4) it throws considerable light on the occasionally obscure writings of Aleister Crowley. 5); it is dedicated to Crowley, who was the Ankh-af-na-Khonsu mentioned in *The Book of the Law*–a dedication which served both as a token of personal loyalty and devotion to Crowley, but was also a gesture of my spiritual independence from him.

In his profound investigation into the origins and basic nature of man, Robert Ardrey in *African Genesis* recently made a shocking statement. Although man has begun the conquest of outer space, the ignorance of his own nature, says Ardrey, "has become institutionalized, universalized and sanctified." He further states that were a brotherhood of man to be formed today, "its only possible common bond would be ignorance of what man is."

Such a condition is both deplorable and appalling when the means are readily available for man to acquire a thorough understanding of himself–and in so doing, an understanding of his neighbor and the world in which he lives as well as the greater Universe of which each is a part.

May everyone who reads this new edition of a *A Garden of Pomegranates* be encouraged and inspired to light his own candle of inner vision and begin his journey into the boundless space that lies within himself. Then, through realization of his true identity, each student can become a lamp unto his own path. And more, Awareness of the Truth of his being will rip asunder the veil of unknowing that has heretofore enshrouded the star he already is, permitting the brilliance of his light to illumine the darkness of that part of the Universe in which he abides.

THE TREE OF LIFE
A Study in Magic
New Falcon Publications, First Edition, 2017

By virtue of the widespread ignorance concerning the sovereign nature of the Divine Theurgy, despite frequent references almost everywhere to the subject of Magic, a gross misunderstanding has been permitted to make its growth during the centuries. Few are there today who would appear to possess even the vaguest idea as to what constituted the high objective of that system considered by the sages of antiquity the Royal Art and the Transcendental Magic. And because there have been even fewer in number prepared to defend to the last its philosophy and disseminate its true principles amongst those found worthy of receiving, the field of war strewn with the mangled reputations of its Magi was relinquished to the charlatans. These, alas, made good use of their opportunity for wholesale despoliation. So much so, that the word Magic itself has now become synonymous with all that is odious, and is conceived to be an obnoxious thing.

For several centuries in Europe was this unrighteous condition of things permitted. It continued for some while until about the middle of the last century, when Eliphas Levi, a writer with a certain facility of expression and a flair for synthesis and surface exposition, endeavoured to restore to Magic its age-old lofty reputation. How his efforts would have fared had not they been succeeded and abetted by the advent of the philosophy of the Theosophical Movement in 1875, together with the open discussion of occult and mystical matters which thereafter ensued, is exceedingly hard to say. Even so, they have been none too successful. For despite nearly eighty long years of attention to and the unconcealed discussion of the esoteric philosophy and practice of various of its branches, there can be found in the Catalogue of the British Museum Reading Room, for instance, no *single work* on Magic which attempts to provide a lucid, unambiguous, and exact exegesis, unhampered by too great an employment of symbol and figure of speech. Eighty years of occult study! And not one serious work on Magic!

For some little while has it been known in various quarters that the writer was a student of Magic. As a consequence enquiries would frequently be addressed to him as to its nature. So numerous did they become as time went on, and so abysmal was the unintentional ignorance of the subject that all displayed, that it seems high time to make available for that public a synthetic and definitive exposition. Inasmuch as no other individual has attempted this task of paramount importance, upon the writer devolves this difficult work. He does not propose to limit himself by specious remarks concerning the incommunicability of occult secrets. Nor will he mention the impossibility of conveying the true nature of the mysteries of ancient time, as some recent authors have done. Though all this is true, nevertheless there is enough in Magic which is communicable. In spite of hundreds of pages to elucidate, against these writers also must be levelled the grim accusation of having done much to confirm public opinion in the already firm belief that Magic was ambiguous, obscure, and fatuous. A greater misconception than this could hardly be held. For Magic, let me insist, is lucid. It is definite and precise. There are no vague formulæ or dubieties comprehended within the sphere of its exactitude; all is clear-cut and devised for practical experiment. Its system is absolutely scientific, and each part thereof is capable of verification and demonstrable proof. *The Tree of Life* is published, somewhat hesitatingly it is true, with the sole object of filling in the existent gap. The writer desires to render intelligible and comprehensible to the ordinary intelligent layman, to the student of the Mysteries and those versed in the lore of other mystical systems and philosophies, the root principles from which the tremendous high-towering structure of Magic is built. With one exception, not known or suitable to the public at large, unfortunately, this necessary task has never previously been accomplished.

The frequency of long quotations from the writings of magical authorities which the writer has inserted herein is quite simply explainable. It was due solely to the desire to demonstrate that the larger essentials of this exposition are not the outcome of any inventiveness of the writer, but are firmly rooted in the wisdom of antiquity. That there are crudities of expression, possible misinterpretations of fact or theory, sins of omission and commission, the writer needs hardly to be informed. By reason thereof he is humbly apologetic. He must be pardoned by virtue of his youth and inexperience. May his efforts spur some other more learned individual, gifted with greater facility of pen, and possessed of a more profound knowledge of the subject and its concomitants, to provide a better formulation of Magic. The writer will be among the first to acclaim it with welcome and eulogy.

It is also necessary to acknowledge the courtesy of Messrs. Methuen & Co. in extending permission to reproduce the illustrations of the four Egyptian Gods from *The Gods of the Egyptians*, by Sir E. A. Wallis Budge.

Israel Regardie
London, *August* 1932.

Dr. Israel Regardie's
Definitive Work on Aleister Crowley's
THE EYE IN THE TRIANGLE
New Falcon Publications, First Edition, 2017

There is a time to speak and a time to remain silent. For me, the time has come now to raise my voice in the interest of clarifying the record of Aleister Crowley. He was one of the greatest mystics of all time, although a very complicated and controversial person. He has too long suffered from misrepresentation and vilification at the hands of uniformed biographers. It is time finally to set the record straight. This must be done, not merely out of regard for the man himself, but even more importantly, because of the profound effect he has had on thousands of readers, and will yet have on countless thousands more.

John Symonds, his major biographer, evinces throughout his narrative a totally contemptuous attitude towards Crowley. This hostility altogether invalidates his attempt at biography. His book The Great Beast could have been excellent since every opportunity in the world was given him through access to diaries and a mass of hitherto unpublished material. Crowley had appointed him executor of his literary estate, and because of this, Symonds had a unique opportunity to set the record straight once and for all. However his personal prejudices got in the way. His writing is cynical, showing no glimmer of insight or the slightest trace of sympathy.

"Crowley was not a great poet," he wrote, "although he wrote a few good poems.... The dominating effect is one of insincerity." He goes on to assert that "in most of his verses there are rarely found those strains which result from a surrender to the poetic moment; instead, he mainly harnessed his talent to his occult interests and personal obsessions which are unsuitable for poetry."[1]

Charles R. Cammell thinks otherwise. His book *Aleister Crowley, the Man, the Mage, the Poet* is a far more telling piece of work. Referring to the three volumes of *Collected Works*, which incidentally is a very early publication, he wrote: "These Works were for the most part poetical, and comprised a mass of poetry which for variety, versatility, range of mood, matter and manner, had absolutely no peer or counterpart in the literature of our time."[2] He also presented a more accurate picture of Crowley as a mystic, though the edge is taken off his otherwise fine presentation by a tendency to moralize, which scotomized him to certain well-ascertained facts. Were one able to combine this volume with that of Symonds, one could form a more adequate conception of the complexity as well as creativity of this man of genius.

He is clearly not a poet to be sneered at, this man who could pen the following from *The World's Tragedy:*

> Hear then! By Abrasax! The bar
> Of the unshifting star
> Is broken — lo! Asar!
> My spirit is wrapt in the wind of light;
> It is whirled away on the wings of night,
> Sable-plumed are the wonderful wings,
> But the silver of moonlight subtly springs
> Into the feathers that flash with the pace

---

[1] *The Great Beast*, John Symonds, Rider & Co., London, 1951, p.35.
[2] *Aleister Crowley, the Man, the Mage, the Poet*, Charles R. Cammell. London, Richards Press, 1951, p.1.

Of our flight to the violate bounds of space.
Time is dropt like a stone from the stars;
Space is a chaos of broken bars:
Being is merged in a furious flood
That rages and hisses and foams in the blood.
See! I am dead! I am passed, I am passed
Out of the sensible world at last.
I am not. Yet I am, as I never was,
A drop in the sphere of molten glass
Whose radiance changes and shifts and drapes
The infinite soul in finite shapes.
There is light, there is life, there is love, there is sense
Beyond speech, beyond song, beyond evidence.
There is wonder intense, a miraculous sun,
As the many are molten and mixed into one
With the heat of its passion; the one hath invaded
The heights of its soul, and it laughter is braided
With the comets whose plumes are the galaxies
Like winds on the night's inaccessible seas...

Or, the mystic who could write tenderly in *The Book of Lapis Lazuli*:

I await Thee in sleeping, in waking. I invoke Thee no more; for Thou art in me, O Thou who hast made me a beautiful instrument tuned to Thy rapture.
Yet art Thou ever apart, even as I.
I remember a certain holy day in the dusk of the year, in the dusk of the Equinox of Osiris, when first I beheld Thee visibly; when first the dreadful issue was fought out; when the Ibis-headed One charmed away that strife.

I remember Thy first kiss, even as a maiden should. Nor in the dark by-ways was there another; Thy kisses abide.

Or, again, in *The Book of the Heart Girl with a Serpent*:

Weary, weary! saith the scribe. Who shall lead me to the sight of the Rapture of my master? The body is weary and the soul is sore weary and sleep weighs down their eyelids; yet ever abides the sure consciousness of ecstasy, unknown, yet known in that its being is certain. O Lord, be my helper, and bring me to the bliss of the Beloved.

All day I sing of Thy delight. All night I delight in Thy song. There is no other day or night than this.

The poet-mystic who could write the following in *Aha!* is surely one to be reckoned with:

> Even so. And One Supreme there is
> Whom I have known, being He. Withdrawn
> Within the curtains of the dawn
> Dwells that concealed. Behold! He is
> A blush, a breeze, a song, a kiss,
> A rosy flame like Love, his eyes
> Blue, the quintessence of all the skies,
> His hair a foam of gossamer
> Pale gold as jasmine, lovelier
> Than all the wheat of Paradise.
> O the dim water-wells his eyes!
> There is such a depth of Love in them
> That the adept is rapt away,
> Dies on that mouth, a gleaming gem
> Of dew caught in the boughs of Day!

Had I a million songs,
And every song a million words,
And every word a million meanings,
I could not count the choral throngs
Of Beauty's beatific birds,
Or gather up the paltry gleanings
Of this great harvest of delight!
Hast thou not heard the words aright?
That world is truly infinite.......

In my wanderings I came
To an ancient park aflame
With fairies' feet. Still wrapped in love
I was caught up, beyond, above
The tides of being. The great sight
Of the intolerable light
Of the whole universe that wove
The labyrinth of life and love
Blazed in me. Then some giant will,
Mine or another's thrust a thrill
Through the great vision. All the light
Went out in an immortal night,
The world annihilated by
The opening of the Master's Eye...

His definition of poetry in the Preface to *The City of God* stems from the deepest beliefs of his life, and compares well with any similar essay:

Poetry is the geyser of the Unconscious.

Poetry is the intelligible musical expression of the Real whose mirror is the phenomenal Universe.

Poetry is the Hermes to lead the "soul" Eurydice from the murk of illusion to the light of Truth; "and on Daedalian oarage fare forth to the interlunar air."

A living poem must effect a definite magical excitement—exaltation in the hearer or reader, similar to the experience of "falling in love at first sight" with a woman. Analysis and argument cannot convince, and may inhibit the reaction, which is above emotion and reason.

The reception of a poem, being a ritual Magical initiation, suffers no interruption...

Daniel P. Mannix's *The Beast* which first appeared in one of the men's sport magazines is a pathetic piece of hack writing, largely a rehash of the Symonds biography but not nearly as well done. I would prefer to ignore this book but since it has appeared in a paperback edition, it is guaranteed a circulation in the thousands. Mannix is completely without comprehension of what Crowley aspired to, and apparently knows his writings only at second hand, which is not good enough for critical evaluation. If he were "a superior American sports writer" as the blurb on the back of the pocket edition indicates, it would have been far better had he stuck to sports reporting.

On page 22 of that book, Mannix refers to me as follows: "The Mysteries of the Golden Dawn have since been published by Mr. Israel Regardie, formerly secretary of the Order, and now a psychologist in California. The Mysteries take up seven thick volumes and I've waded through most of them."

In these few lines, he has made several errors. At no time had I been the secretary of the Golden Dawn, nor had I ever held any office in that Order. I had served as Crowley's secretary for some years, but this was a generation or more *after* he had severed his own connection with the Order. Nor was I a psychologist per se, though I had taken four years of chiropractic training in New York and psychoanalytic training of many hundreds of clinical hours in London, New York and Los Angeles. Ultimately, I came to practice within the confines of the chiropractic profession, as manipulative form of psychotherapy based on the work of Wilhelm Reich. These facts would have been easy for Mannix to verify had he made even the slightest effort. Finally, my book *The Golden Dawn* was published in four volumes, not in seven as he states.

It seems to me then that if Mannix, referring to me, could make this many mistakes within a few lines, his views about Crowley expressed in over a hundred pages are very much open to question. He does not recommend himself as an apostle of accuracy.

Finally, there is Gilbert Highet, a radio commentator who has "captured a wide, literate audience during recent years," according to the blurb on the back of his book *Talents and Geniuses* (New York, Meridian Books Inc., 1959) It also avers that he "here displays his varied interests, his wit, his erudition in discussions of topics ranging from Bach to Zen Buddhism."

Highet offers an essay on Crowley which begins with a review of Somerset Maugham's *The Magician*. From this he concludes that Crowley was not a *fake* as some people have been led to believe, but a *failure*. In opposition to Christianity, which is essentially sex-negative, Crowley had wished to establish a solar-phallic religion (a felicitous phrase borrowed from Jung's *Psychology of the Unconscious*). He had in mind a type of worship which would be rooted in man's deepest biological and spiritual needs. Highet says this kind of religion obviously has not succeeded in spreading to any extent—therefore, Crowley has failed.

Superficially, this comment is valid. Nevertheless we have to remember that the early preaching of the Gospels was not a starling success for a considerable time. Actually some scholars wonder if it ever really succeeded in making anything but the most trivial impact on the everyday lives of most people. It took centuries of violence and bloodshed to convert the masses to Christianity. Crowley has been dead less than a score of years. Who can estimate how many hundreds or even thousands of people have been influenced in one way or another by his writing?

There is no solar-phallic church to spread his gospel. But it is not impossible that time may take care of this too. Stranger things have happened![3]

Highet then continues his irrational criticism of Crowley by stating that "he was a failure...He poured forth an interminable torrent of bad poetry, meaningless prose, and amateurish drawings and paintings."

If they are meaningless to Highet, it only exposes his own prejudice. In a later essay on Zen, he is able to explore the subject with some semblance of empathy and insight, but he could not approach Crowley without suspicion and perhaps jealousy, because Crowley was a far greater writer.

"He would not study," wrote Highet presumptuously flying in the face of well-established facts, "but preferred to evoke visions and oracles from his own subconscious, which anyone can do."

I suppose this is the same kind of vicious criticism that must have once assailed William Blake, whose poetry, visions and apocalyptic writings are now integrally imbedded in English literature—as I predict will much of the literary output of Crowley in time to come. If Highet had become acquainted with some of the contents of his own Unconscious, it might have spared him of the ignominy of placing on record derogatory statements which ultimately will be his own judge and accuser. If *anyone* can evoke at will visions and oracles from the depths of his self, as Highet claims, all I can say is that this runs counter to my professional experience of more than twenty-five years. Most people are cut off from the roots in the unconscious psyche.

---

[3] *The Berkeley Barb*, of San Francisco, in its issue of September 4, 1969, seems determined to make Gilbert Highet eat his words, as well as to fulfil my own prediction. The illustration on the front page of that issue would have set all of Crowley's tissues ablaze.

For these and other reasons, then, I decided to reexamine the life of this literary and mystical genius to see if in the light of my own personal experience and understanding, it may not be possible to unravel some of the twisted skeins of which Crowley was fashioned. There are certain well-defined influences so outstanding that I fail to see why they have not been better exploited. They may not wholly explain him—any more than I think any person may be wholly explained, psychoanalysis notwithstanding. But perhaps some of his deep, underlying motivations may be evoked and scrutinized so that we can see what they are and how they affected him. Some of them are clear, and these I propose in the following pages to explore and delineate, for they seem to help us understand what manner of man this was. For this was a man who has written immortally. We must keep that writing alive. It may be that what he did and what he wrote are vitally important for all of us. Flippancy and cynicism do nothing for him any more than they do for us. Something more is required to reveal the goals we are striving towards.

THE PHILOSOPHER'S STONE
New Falcon Publications, First Edition, 2018

During the winter of 1936-37, while living in London, I came down with a severe cold which proved intractable to treatment. My respiratory tract had become sensitized in early childhood by a bout of bilateral bronchial pneumonia. The result was that I was confined to bed for two weeks.

Instead of the usual mystery and detective stories recommended for such situations, my reading companion was Mrs. Atwood's *Suggestive Inquiry into the Hermetic Mystery*. For years I had struggled vainly with this large tome, annoyed continually by its obscurantism and pompous literary style that was almost as bad as A. E. Waite's, but I had never really managed to comprehend her presentation of Alchemy. Now, bedridden, I was determined to give her book one final perusal. If, then, it still yielded nothing for me, I proposed to discard it along with some other books which had outlived their usefulness in my life. So, with notebook and pencil by my side in bed, I began casually to glance through Mrs. Atwood's book, underlining a significant passage here and there, and jotting down some brief notes on the pad.

Suddenly, and to my utter amazement, the whole enigma became crystal clear and alive. The formerly mysterious *Golden Tractate of Hermes* and *The Six Keys of Eudoxus* seemed all at once to open up to unfold their meaning. Feverishly, I wrote. In effect, the greater part of *The Philosopher's Stone* got written in those two weeks of bronchitis. It is true that later I added some diagrams together with a short commentary to Vaughan's alchemical text, and a few quotations from Carl G. Jung and other authors whose works were not immediately available while I was confined to bed. But actually the main body of the book was composed there and then.

My book has been praised as a good meaningful book by some reviewers and by many readers, to judge from the mail I have received during the past thirty years. It is patently an open sesame to one level of interpretation. *The Occult Review*, now defunct, published a critical review by Archibald Cockren who took me rather severely to task for asserting that alchemical texts should be interpreted solely in terms of psychological and mystical terms. He himself, I subsequently discovered, had written a book *Alchemy Rediscovered and Restored*. Of course, I immediately procured a copy. Since I was peeved by his review, I did not feel that his book had very much to offer—so I dismissed both offhand. I was about to write the editor of *The Occult Review* a scorching letter, but reason intervened so that fortunately it never got written.

The opportunity is rarely given to an author in his lifetime "to eat crow" and to enjoy it. This lot, it pleases me to say, is mine—after thirty years. Not that I would significantly change much of what I wrote then. I admitted that I had not "proceeded to the praxis" but I felt then and still do that a mystical and psychological interpretation of some alchemical texts was legitimate. There is unequivocally this aspect of the subject. Certainly Jacob Boehme and Henry Khunrath, for example, cannot be interpreted except in these terms.

Nor should one be permitted to forget some of the preliminary provisions laid down by Basil Valentine in *The Triumphant Chariot of Antimony*:

This object I pursue not only for the honour and glory of the Divine Majesty, but also in order that men may render to God implicit obedience in all things.

I have found that in this Meditation there are five principal heads, which must be diligently considered, as much are in possession of the wisdom of philosophy as by all who aspire after that wisdom which is attained in our art. The first is the invocation of God; the second, the contemplation of Nature; the third, true preparation; the fourth, the way of using; the fifth, the use and profit. He who does not carefully attend to these points will never be included among real Alchemists, or be numbered among the perfect professors of the Spagyric science. Therefore, we will treat of them in their proper order as lucidly and succinctly as we can, in order that the careful and studious operator may be enabled to perform our Magistery in the right way.

It is evident then that though some alchemists did work manually in a chemical laboratory, they were at the same time men of the highest spiritual aspirations. For them, the Stone was not only tangible evidence of successful metallic transmutations; it was accompanied by an equivalent spiritual transmutatory process.

My readers will know by now that my thinking on most of these occult subjects had been profoundly influenced by the life and work of Aleister Crowley. So far as his knowledge of alchemy went, I ought to narrate that in the winter of 1897, he had gone to Switzerland for mountain-climbing and winter sports. While there he encountered a Julian Baker with whom he had a long conversation about alchemy. This indicates at the very least that Crowley had been widely reading on this topic as well as on mysticism. As a result of this conversation, Baker promised to introduce Crowley to a chemist in London, George Cecil Jones, who might be instrumental in getting him admitted into the Hermetic Order of the Golden Dawn. There is not the least shred of evidence to indicate that Crowley, Baker or Jones had done any practical laboratory work in alchemy. In magic–yes; in alchemy, no!

Many years later, Crowley came to use alchemical symbolism to elucidate the "Mass of the Holy Ghost", the sex-magic principles of the O.T.O., principles which I re-stated in the 16th chapter of *The Tree of Life*.

To refer back to the Golden Dawn, it seems to me that there was little that was really illuminating on alchemy in its curriculum, though in other areas, particularly the magical, I feel to-day as I always have.

The Golden Dawn was essentially a Qabalistic and magical order, not an alchemical one. I do not know of any evidence pointing out that Mathers or Westcott had ever engaged in operating an alchemical laboratory. One document bearing the imprimatur of Mathers deals with alchemy, not from the laboratory viewpoint, but from that of ritual magic–and at best it is plain verbiage. Its mystical interpretation is best expressed in a speech made by one Adept in its classic ritual: "In the alembic of thine heart, through the athanor of affliction, seek thou the True Stone of the Wise."

To this extent, the Golden Dawn had severed its traditional ties with the parent Rosicrucian bodies of Germany and Central Europe which were patently alchemical. One has only to glance casually through *The Secret Symbols of the Rosicrucians* to realize the extent to which Alchemy was considered the predominant feature in the Rosicrucian work of that era.

I know none of its members who could at any time have thrown any ray of light on alchemy. One member, the late Capt. J. Langford Garstin, wrote a couple of books, *Theurgy and The Secret Fire*, about alchemy, but they too yield little of practical value on the subject. I have met people here and there in the past forty years who could talk about Alchemy, but I cannot say that any of them made much sense.

Events in the past few years–a Uranus cycle–have conspired to force upon me a thoroughgoing expansion or reorientation of my original point of view, so that I can now quite happily admit that Archibald Cockren was right.

How this came about is a story in itself–typical of the way in which such things occur. Through a friend of a friend of mine, I was introduced to Mr. Albert Riedel of Salt Lake City, Utah, while he was visiting Los Angeles. At the time, I was domiciled there, enjoying the sunny climate and occasionally ruminating over the inclement weather of London where I was born. It took only a few minutes to realize that I was talking to the first person I had *ever* met who *knew* what he was talking about on the subject of Alchemy. We promised to keep in touch–and we did.

This promise later eventuated in an invitation to attend a seminar on Alchemy that he was conducting at the newly instituted Paracelsus Research Society in Salt Lake City. Most of the material presented in the Seminar concerned Alchemy, Qabalah, Astrology, *etc.*–with which I was already theoretically familiar–though even there some radically new and stimulating viewpoints were obtained. But the *piece-de-resistance* was the laboratory work. Here, I was wholly dumbfounded.

It took no more than a few minutes to help me realize how presumptuous I had been to assert dogmatically that all alchemy was psycho-spiritual. What I witnessed there, and have since repeated, has sufficed to enable me to state categorically that, in insisting solely on a mystical interpretation of alchemy, I had done a grave disservice to the ancient sages and philosophers.

When Basil Valentine said, for example, in his work on antimony: "Take the best Hungarian Antimony...pulverize it as finely as possible, spread thinly on an earthenware dish (round or square)...

place the dish on a calcinatory furnace over a coal fire..." he means exactly what he says–exactly and literally. When he says a coal fire, he was not referring to the inner fire or Kundalini. It is simply ridiculous to assume he is talking in symbols which must be interpreted metaphysically, *etc*. Once you have followed his instructions to the letter, literally, or have been privileged to have seen this laboratory process demonstrated, then you know that "manually" is certainly not meant to be interpreted as by Mrs. Atwood in terms of mesmeric passage of the hands.

There is a more or less lengthy passage in Praxis *Spagyrica Philosophica* by Frater Albertus (Salt Lake City, 1966) which is worthy of quotation at this juncture. He wrote, in a footnote to page 77 *et seq*:

> Some have gone to extreme pains to duplicate the ancient implements of former alchemists. They had to be able to obtain better, or at least for sure, the same results with our modern instruments. Take the regulation of heat alone. Formerly, it was an arduous task requiring an assistant to keep the temperatures under control for the various manipulations. This expense alone was one that not many of the average persons could afford. Today we have gas, natural or artificial, electricity and other means at our disposal giving us a much greater accuracy than was possible to obtain by manual operation. Vessels are stronger and not as fragile as formerly. Pyrex and similar glass containers can take much more heat and are in less danger of breaking. Stainless steel, another of the modern marvels, does away with the old copper still that had formerly many corrosive sublimates and other by-products when natural processes were followed...
>
> Last, but not least, it should be remembered that many of the essential ingredients used had to be prepared by slow

and sometimes hard manual operations. The required basic substances were not always as easily available as it appears. Great distances, and the necessary time involved, made it even more difficult. There was no air parcel post. Horse drawn wagons had to bring the goods that were not immediately available (sometimes from foreign countries). No telephone calls over greater distances, spanning continents, were available to make possible the information needed at a critical point...Despite all these and similar hardships they were able to accomplish what many in our days cannot do. Telephone and air travel not withstanding...

Again, let me repeat, my analysis of the three alchemical texts of *The Philosopher's Stone* is worth preserving. I am glad that it has returned to print in a new edition. I should have re-written parts of the book in order to incorporate what I have since discovered through the person and work of Frater Albertus Spagyricus, the *non-de-plume* which he prefers to be known by, but I have decided to let it stand as it was first written.

It did represent the dawn of insight for me then, and it was the product of a genuine illumination, partial though it was, and outgrown it as I have today. As such, I think it is the inherent right to continued existence in its original form. Moreover, it may prove useful to other students who have not yet discovered this point of view, which certainly is a valid one. They may be at the stage of growth I was in thirty years ago, where it could be of value. It needs merely to be supplemented by other reading of more recent vintage.

In the meantime, *The Philosopher's Stone* with these preliminary comments, should answer a wide-felt need which has called forth this new edition. I hope, being in print once more, it will bring new light and knowledge and values to present-day students who may be still groping in the dark areas of the occult towards alchemy, where a guiding hand needs to be extended.

So, to close this Introduction, I must use the ancient Rosicrucian greeting, and the close of a Golden Dawn ritual:

> May what we have partaken here sustain us in our search for the Quintessence; the Stone of the Philosophers, True Wisdom and perfect Happiness, the Summum Bonum.
>
> Valete, Fratres et Sorores.
> Roseae Rubeau et Aureae Crucis.
> Benedictus Dominus Deus noste quidedit nobis hoc signum.

Israel Regardie

Studio City, California
November 1, 1968

THE LEGEND OF ALEISTER CROWLEY
New Falcon Publications, Fourth Revised Edition, 2015

It was in the Spring of the year 1929 that the Sûreté Générale sprang a surprise on the unsuspecting Crowley menage. Aleister Crowley was living in Paris with his mistress, Marie de Miramar. I had moved from a small hotel nearby into the apartment on Avenue de Suffren in the *XVI* arrondissement, serving as his secretary. We were all handed expulsion papers. Leave within twenty-four hours!

Crowley immediately pleaded illness to gain time to institute legal proceedings of some kind to reverse the expulsion. De Miramar and I had no recourse but to follow the terms of the *Refus de Sejour* and we wound up in Brussels to await the arrival of Crowley.

Finally realizing that there was no shaking the intransigeant attitude of the Sûreté Générale, he cast off the dust of Paris from his shoes. In Brussels, he was persuaded to join some of his fervent disciples in Berlin. The problem was how to get both de Miramar and myself there.

Having been expelled from France and refused admittance to England (as narrated at some length in *The Eye in the Triangle*), we all had serious doubts about the German authorities permitting us entry. So Crowley decided to marry de Miramar, thinking that would facilitate her entry into Germany. But that wasn't easy in Brussels; so much red tape surrounded a marriage of foreigners on Belgian soil. But since the subject of marriage had been raised, it persisted despite the difficulties raised by the Belgians. He took a chance on taking de Miramar with him to Berlin to get married there. The chance paid off. I was to stay on in Brussels typing an additional set of copies of *The Confessions* for ultimate publication. This was forty years ago!

After a successful summer in Berlin, Crowley and his wife returned to England. This time there was no problem about her admission, since she had married a Briton. While in London, he met the proprietors of the Mandrake Press on Museum Street. One of them, P. R. Stephensen, had previous experience in the book business, having run the Fanfrolico Press a bit earlier with a writer named James Lindsay, I believe, producing some handsomely printed, bound and illustrated books. He became so enthusiastic over much of Crowley's writing that he persuaded his partner, named Goldston or Goldstein, I cannot remember which, to start a publishing program of Crowley's works. In quick succession, *The Stratagem, Moonchild,* and the first two volumes of a projected six volume set of *The Confessions of Aleister Crowley* came off the press.

While this publishing program was under way, Crowley, who was far from a well man, moved out of London to a little town in Kent named Knockholt. Stephensen rented a house there. I imagine it was Stephensen who persuaded Crowley to rent a house there also. This was to facilitate possible discussion relative to the Crowley publication program.

I managed to gain entry into England towards the end of the year 1929, perhaps in November, and immediately joined Crowley in Knockholt, about thirty miles or so south of London. There I found Crowley ill with a severe bout of phlebitis, while Marie suffered with colitis, boredom and loneliness, and excessive drinking.

We all suffered from boredom in Knockholt. To relieve this, Crowley and I played chess a good deal. I managed to have time to read every book and manuscript I could lay hands on that Crowley had written. In this manner, I have acquired an almost encyclopedic view of Crowley's literary output. Marie coped with her boredom not only through the ingestion of alcohol, but by painting with oils, a pretty messy and unproductive business.

It was not a serene household by any means. Every now and again, I succeeded in getting out of the house, walking down the street to where the Stephensen's lived. I never knew what P. R. stood for, but Winifred, his wife, called him Inky—and Inky he was to all of us. They were very charming and kind people, and I spent many a pleasant hour and even afternoon there, playing chess with Inky, talking a great deal, and receiving the benefit of their generous Australian hospitality.

Inky's interest in Aleister Crowley was wholly literary. He had a good grounding in philosophy, but cared absolutely nothing for the occult. He was amusedly tolerant of my interest in magick and yoga and inner growth and development, but it was without serious meaning to him. He was a good-natured, kind, generous human being who enjoyed living, mental stimulation, good food and drink, sex, and fine literature, especially if the latter had been produced in beautiful editions.

Meantime, it seems as though the Mandrake Press was running into a great deal of stiff opposition from the booksellers both in London and England as a whole. They wanted nothing to do with Crowley. His reputation had been thoroughly blackened by the exposé conducted by James Douglas in the *Sunday Express* years earlier when Collins first published Crowley's *Diary of a Drug Fiend*. His expulsion from Italy did his reputation no good, nor was the recent expulsion from France any great help. Sales were poor, and Goldstein was getting worried. After all, he had put up the capital, and there was not much of a return.

This put Stephensen in a very awkward position. He was still enthused about the excellent quality of Crowley's writing, and wanted to continue publishing. He and Crowley discussed this at some length. Since, in Crowley's home, there was the big scrap-book of press reviews and notices, it struck Inky that Mandrake's selling position might be enhanced if he compiled a book using these book-reviews as a defense of Crowley against current sales resistance.

Inky was a good writer. He had done a great deal of ghost-writing both before and after this particular book *The Legend*. In fact, a couple of years afterwards, when Crowley had wandered off to Germany again, I helped Inky in his ghosting of two other books—one on the life of Anna Pavlova by her former musical director, and another on fox-hounds and fox-hunting by a master of hounds in South Kent. This was fun. I learned a lot from him for which I am most indebted. I hope, wherever he is, he may read this so that he can learn of my appreciation and gratitude to him.

Crowley, as it were, loaned me to Stephensen to help him with the proposed book. Inky had the skill of the writer. Crowley had the scrap-book. I had the broad familiarity with Crowely's writing. So Inky went to work dictating to me with my Stenotype. We worked daily and steadfastly.

I cannot recall now how long it actually took to write this book, but it was not very long. Months previously I had been asked to make a précis of Crowley's lengthy article "The Last Straw" originally published in *The International* when he was the editor during the War years. It was included in the text of

The Legend. When completed it served as a splendid recapitulation of Crowley's literary reception by the British and world press. Inky used the scrapbook to superb advantage, working into it both favorable and adverse criticisms so that a colorful tapestry was woven, proving to the British booksellers how utterly mistaken they were in showing antagonism to this new Crowley release. It turned out to be a good book. Even today, forty years after the event, it still reads well and so deserves to be re-issued.

However, in 1930, when it first came out, it reluctantly sold out a small first edition—and that was the end. It never really got off the ground. Nor did it eradicate the booksellers' refusal to handle Crowley. The Mandrake Press went down the drain.

Goldstein got fed up and pulled out from the Mandrake Press; the partnership was dissolved. It was invested in by some Crowley disciples who then took in a couple of ex-Army men who professed to be financiers. Under their able jurisdiction, the poor Mandrake Press was first incorporated and, shortly afterwards, liquidated.

Inky withdrew to Knockholt, did some more ghosting, and ultimately returned to Australia, his native land. Many years afterwards, I received a letter from him relative to Crowley, still demonstrating his high regard for the latter's literary work. Inky never fell out with Crowley as had so many of the latter's friends and associates. The contact had been too short really. Inky was able to retain his high regard and respect for the "old man" as we familiarly called him.

This is 1969. The world has changed a great deal since then. The hippies have come—but not quite gone. In the meantime, they have left an indelible impress on our culture. Part of this impress bears all the earmarks of a Crowley revival. The result is a vast interest in Crowley's books which now command a high premium, money wise, when they are at all possible to obtain—which is not very often. Most of those who own Crowley literature usually hang on to it, but little of it finding its way to used bookstores.

Crowley died in 1947. Why he appointed John Symonds as one of his literary executors is a mystery that never will be divined. It is perhaps another example of Crowley's poor judgment about people. Symonds wrote a disgusting book over a decade ago entitled *The Great Beast*. It is a malicious, contemptible piece of work crammed with deliberate misinterpretation and ignorant misunderstanding of what Crowley stood for. This wretched work was followed by another, *The Magick of Aleister Crowley*. In this second book, Symonds has extrapolated from the diaries and other works by Crowley in such a contemptible manner as to make "the old man" look like a complete idiot.

Not content with this insolence, Symonds has steadfastly refused permission to me and several other writers to use any of Crowley's published material. Evidently, he has assumed that his literary executorship, instituted on behalf of and for the benefit of the Ordo Templi Orientis, should be used for his own personal gain. Recently, he has written an introduction to *The Confessions* just published in England by Jonathan Cape Ltd., and which will be published early in 1970 in the United States by Hill & Wang Inc. This introduction shows a modification of his earlier stand on Crowley. While not at all complimentary, it is not so devastatingly critical of Crowley. I have to admit that his editing of *The Confessions* is not bad. For this he needs some little applause—but not too much.

I have suggested to Llewellyn Publications that this *Legend of Aleister Crowley* be republished because the English reviews of *The Confessions* show that the old intransigeant attitude towards Crowley has not altered throughout the years. He is still regarded as the "bad boy of English journalism." Curiously enough, I have just received a letter from a psychiatrist friend in England who recently read *The Confessions*, about which he could only remark:

> I am struck by Crowley's brilliance, the vividness of his thought, his picturesque language, his great sense of humour, the energy that he put into life—in fact, there is more than a bit of manic restlessness in his make-up. But what is the difference anyway—between mild and well-controlled manic energy and healthy enthusiasm?

This professional point of view is worth remembering as I follow Inky's original example to quote from some contemporary reviewers of *The Confessions of Aleister Crowley*.

The Times Literary Supplement dated 23 October 1969, had a very long review of the book, which would have pleased Crowley no end. It appeared on the first page, running over onto the second. The review, without a byline, says:

> The reader may thus approach Crowley himself either as Ipsissimus, the incarnation of the Logos of the New Aeon, or as a human enigma.

It then proceeds quite fairly to enumerate some of the egotistical extravagances of Crowley in these words:

> He was dazzled by his multi-faceted brilliance. With Oscar Eckenstein, he shared the glory of being superior to all other mountaineers. He was a master of chess (half-blue at Cambridge). He was the equal of Shakespeare as a poet, a novelist and shorty-story writer of sublimity, a traveller in the physical and spiritual worlds as adventurous as Sir Richard Burton, a psychologist more profound than his coeval Freud, a scientific magician in the tradition of the greatest masters but humbly their superior because he had been chosen by the gods through his Holy Guardian Angel to initiate the new Aeon of God the Child. He was an aristocrat, knighted by Don Carlos, etc., etc.,

The rest of the review is taken up with exposing some of his less admirable character traits, terminating with:

> The authorities, and the general public, viewed Crowley with justifiable mistrust. He was as much the epitome of all disharmony and confusion as the demon Chronozon of his evocation. He was mad, bad, and dangerous to know. But this was not because he was deliberately evil. It was something far more sinister and dangerous. The Logos of the New Aeon, he sincerely believed that, having crossed the Abyss, he was beyond good and evil; and frankly he didn't give a damn for the whole human race. They were nothing but a pack of cards.

What a Joker he was!

In the whole two page review, there is not one single line to be construed as favorable to Crowley's work or reputation. It is a lengthy denunciation, veiled certainly, but just as destructive in its own way as were the original full page editorial ravings of James Douglas in *The Sunday Express*.

The Listener of the same date is hardly more complimentary. The reviewer, whose name is D. J. Enright, begins with an anecdote about a second-hand bookstore where he had picked up a book by Conrad which bore Crowley's autograph on the flyleaf. It had been marked down several times, leading him to comment:

> The declining market-value of Crowley's autograph indicates the low esteem into which he had fallen before his death in 1947. This 'autohagiography' is unlikely to establish him as anything more than another English Eccentric, *fin-de-siecle* variety, graded unsuitable for promotion by the British Council.

Maybe! So far as the declining market-value of Crowley's books are concerned, let me put on record the fact that many years ago a set of the *Equinox* might be obtained for $100 for the ten volumes. Since all my Crowley books were burgled from my home at the end of February 1969, a local bookseller offered me a week ago the first volume of the *Equinox* for $45,000!

Enright does try to be fair. For example, he wrote:

> Crowley is by no means a figure of fun, and much of this book (though far from all its 1,000 pages) is extremely readable. Besides being many other and different things, he was a bit of a John Bull, a man of common sense and forthright response, with a British contempt for British hypocrisy. He was a tireless and fearless traveller, especially in the East, refusing to avail himself of the advice and assistance customarily proferred by HM Consuls, and like many other Britons he considered the Mohammedans vastly superior to all other brands of native life. Like many other Britons too, he only began to warm to the Chinese when a mandarin invited him to a banquet at which "the opulence of Trimalchio was concealed beneath the refinement of Lucullus and the culture of Horace." Rather less Britishly, he admired the coolies because their performance proved the harmlessness of opium. "I timed the men under the worst conditions and they did eight miles without rest in two hours dead. If those men were 'physical wreaks from the abuse of opium' I should like to see the animal in his undamaged state!"

Regarding Crowley's mountain-climbing exploits in Switzerland, Mexico and India, the reviewer was forced to add:

> It seems that he really was a serious and an intrepid climber. The general reader, with a salt-sprinkler to hand, will find this part of his story, along with his travels, the most palatable—and the chapters on Magick the least palatable, if only because human kind cannot bear very much unreality.

On the whole, Enright is pretty just, commenting fairly accurately on direct quotations from Crowley's book with regard to Liber Legis, his relations with women, and his patronizing attitude towards his disciples and followers.

But the sheer arrogance which makes Crowley's confessions initially so readable begins to pall. A revealing story concerns Victor Neuburg, one of his most faithful followers, who later achieved a rather less ambiguous fame as the discoverer of Dylan Thomas, whose early poems he printed in *The Sunday Referee*...

> As the book goes on, and Crowley becomes increasingly involved in the occult, so it grows increasingly repellent...While Crowley continues with little self-pity to represent himself as a genius misunderstood, he displays his closest associates as unequivocally squalid or foolish, as weaklings, drunkards, drug-addicts, swindlers, pimps, perverts....Perhaps the world is fortunate in that he felt nothing but contempt for secular politics.

There was another review entitled "Emperor of Hocus-Pocus" under the byline of Maurice Richardson which appeared in *The Observer Review* on the 26 October 1969. This is wholly unfavorable and critical all the way through. Its tenor can best be appreciated by a single remark in the first column:

> Sensation-seekers will get better value as well as a clearer, more rounded account in John Symond's biography "The Great Beast".

About the middle of the review there is another paragraph which is indicative further of the general contemptuous attitude which this reviewer shares with John Symonds:

> It is always difficult with megalomaniacal cranks to sort out fantasy and trickery from genuine delusion. It is particularly difficult in Crowley's case because he was not only manic and paranoid and often drugged to the eyes, but also an accomplished con-man....

The concluding sentence of the review is:

> His great gas-bag of an ego which, like a true mystic, he thought he had annihilated, must have been a fearful inconvenience.

The Evening News of October 23, 1969 published a three column review headed in large black type by "A Beastly hard road to fame...." This appeared above a picture of Crowley taken from Equinox III, under which were two lines: "But Crowley would be glad he's not forgotten."

It, too, felt that John Symonds' cynical biography was far more informative and accurate than *The Confessions*. The tenor of the rest of the review can be deduced from that one piece of information.

The reviewer opened his dissertation with several lines in large type:

> Glowering from between Mae West and an Indian guru in that spoof group photograph on the Sgt. Pepper's Lonely Hearts Club Band L.P. is a face with lard-like jowls and hot staring eyes. He looks furious at being there—the Great Beast cut down to Beatle size.

Later, he states:

> He was a flamboyant showman and probably a blackmailer. He was a con-man on a splendid scale.... What is quickly apparent from the bombastic rigmarole is that the Beast was dotty.

It's concluding remark is:

> Doubtless the Beast will be remembered for a long time, so I suppose his ambition came true. But it seems a beastly hard way to have achieved it.

So much for *The Evening News*.

The People, on the same date, published a review with enormous black capital letters under the byline of Tom Driberg. "The most Evil Man on Earth!" But this merely is a quotation from an earlier issue of *John Bull*, as Stephensen has shown in the text of *The Legend*.

Driberg is far from being altogether antagonistic, and seems capable of objective criticism and examination of matters in which he is not especially interested. For example:

His basic commandment was "Do what thou wilt." Since his training in serious, formal magick (as he spelt it) was rigorous, he did not mean by this "Follow each casual impulse." He meant "Discover your own true will and do it." In other words, "Know yourself and be yourself."

But such teaching is easily misunderstood and used as an excuse by the vicious or weak-minded—and Crowley...always had a few of them around.

I first met Crowley when I was very young. He had asked me to lunch in London. I was curious, but distinctly on my guard....The man I met was elderly, bald, stout, and dressed in good green Harris tweeds,—not at all exotic, except that, as we sat down, he said "Pardon me while I invoke the moon."

Indeed, whenever I met him, he seemed normal and worldly—often worried about money, smoking Havana cigars or a pipe, a witty and congenial companion. It was hard to believe all the horrifying stories about him.... Crowley's funeral in 1947, at a municipal crematorium in Sussex, was as unusual as his life had been. Egyptian gods were invoked; Crowley's Hymn to Pan was recited.

The local councillors were deeply disturbed, and resolved that such a thing must not happen again.

I don't suppose it will.

Pat Williams in *The Sunday Telegraph* of October 26, 1969 has perhaps the most interesting, objective, and in many ways the most fair review of the lot. The opening paragraph is actually the theme of this introduction to *The Legend*, that the past dies very hard. People do not relinquish their impressions or memories of past events very readily.

The name of Aleister Crowley—the self-styled 'Beast 666'—still seems to evoke Satanic images 50-odd years after the heavy-breathing Press revelations of orgies and black masses in respectable metropolitan London.

Those images and revelations are going to haunt the public for a very long time, as well as to distort the reputation that Crowley really deserves.

The reviewer is lucid and insightful. Regarding the Law of Thelema, he asks:

> But what is will and whose is the law? The answer, on the evidence here, reveals a far higher intention than one might have expected. Crowley sought to align himself with hidden truths; the phrase was aimed, he says, at getting people to realise their essential selves, where they and the Godhead are one....

Which is not a bad commentary at all!

In Crowley, the braggart smothers the worshipper, the performer masks the priest, the wise man is not so much child as *enfant terrible*. Suicide and insanity were part of the wake he left in his magical and sexual (which were often identical) endeavours.

Yet one emerges even with a respect for his aspiration, his capacity, his hard work and his dedication, and there are things one can take from him.

Just prior to this respectful admission, there is an honest confession which says much for the reviewer. One could wish that many of the other reviewers had been able to accept this as simply as did Pat Williams.

> After nearly 1,000 pages I still don't know what to think of him.

And towards the end of the two column review, there is this final statement:

...a tale written with such conceit, flamboyance, panache, and energetic self-delight that it takes one's breath away.... That still leaves 500 further pages of contemporary gossip, mountaineering and travelling adventures...making it an appalling, fascinating read if you can stomach such swashbuckling swankiness.

Finally, on a note of almost despair, let me call attention to a notice which appeared in *The Psychic News* of November 1, 1969, written by Maurice Barbanell, one of the British stalwarts of the Spiritualist Movement. The notice, which is not a review, is headed 'Clown of the Occult'. I need only to quote a couple of very short paragraphs to give the reader the full flavor of Barbanell's liberal and enlightened attitudes:

> H. D. Ziman, whose review (in *The Daily Telegraph*) was headed 'Clown of the Occult' said that one of the troubles with this megalomaniac was that people were uncertain whether he meant to be taken seriously...
>
> The new book describes how he varied lechery with taking immense does of drugs. I am sure that I don't want to read it.

It will be interesting to observe what will happen when Hill and Wang Inc., bring out the American edition of *The Confessions* early in 1970. At no time in his long career did Crowley ever succeed in making anything but the most superficial impression on English letters or the occult public. When he was domiciled in the U.S. during World War I, unfortunately, it seems that the American literary scene and the American occult-reading public were even less affected by him than was England. It galled him no end. He became much more bitter and vitriolic about the U.S. than ever he had been about his native land, although admittedly a vast amount of his early poetry did condemn the narrowness and bigotry of the British people.

A great deal of what Crowley had to say in *The Confessions* about the United States is so evidently prejudicial, critical and destructive that it can easily be predicted that most of the American reviewers will have a field day. Probably they will seize upon some of these opinions to construct a monstrous reduplication of the aberrant English attitudes of fifty years ago. The current English reviews, as extrapolated above, will be as nothing to what we are likely to read when the American journalists get hold of *The Confessions*. I am far from happy about this prospect.

Admittedly Crowley was a show-off, an egotist, and an *enfant terrible*, as all the reviewers have indicated. But, with only an exception or two, they decline to perceive another aspect of the man which was a great mystic, sincere dedicated and hard working. He made demands on his students that in reality were not nearly as tough as those he made on himself—as the biography has shown. The reviewers became repelled by his self-adulation. Unfortunately, this prevented them from realizing that he really was a great poet, not necessarily the greatest as he claimed, nor on the same level as Shakespeare, but certainly a poet who has penned some immortal lines.

There is indeed ground for criticism of him. However, there is also ground for high praise of some of the things he has done. It is about time that the scale was struck and a balance achieved. For all too long—due in part to his own stupidity as perceived by Pat Williams in the lines "the braggart smothers the worshipper, the performer masks the priest, the wise man is not so much child as *enfant terrible*"— he has been wholly ignored and cruelly vilified. One has to agree with Stephensen that this history of vilification is without equal in literary history.

Despite everything, I am confident that the issuance of *The Confessions*, this *Legend of Aleister Crowley* and my own attempt at biography *The Eye in the Triangle* will accomplish some degree of restitution. They may do a little to right the wrong that has been done to a man of letters, a significantly religious though unorthodox man, a strong and valiant man, and restore him to the high place in history that he deserves.

Israel Regardie

December 15, 1969
Studio City, California

UNDOING YOURSELF
With Energized Meditation and Other Devices
By Dr. Christopher S. Hyatt
New Falcon Publications, First Edition, 1982

Systems of meditation come and go–and have since time immemorial. But somehow meditation is more popular today and I fancy practised by more people than ever before in the world's history. My contention is that this is largely due to the psychedelic movement initiated by Aldous Huxley's *Doors of Perception* and the fantastically pioneering work of Timothy Leary. Posterity, I am certain will have a finer appreciation of what he has contributed to this world than we have today.

Meditation is meditation. But there are innumerable techniques for achieving the proper results. One of the most dynamic that has appeared in recent years is not Transcendental Meditation by the grinning-giggling monkey face guru, though perhaps this is the most popular, but the so-called chaotic meditation of Bhagwan Shree Rajineesh. This is one that really comes nearest to the vital and powerful method described by our author Christopher S. Hyatt. Without equivocation, it can truthfully be stated that this method is by far and away about the best method I have encountered in all my years of both psychotherapy and in the occult world.

As Alan Watts pointed out a long time ago, most Western psychotherapy is fundamentally metaphysical–that is, it is essentially conceptual and verbal. Whereas Eastern "psychotherapy" is more realistically somatically oriented–*viz,* Yoga in all its facets and branches. To this extent the latter is more holistic than the metaphysical approach of the West. (An unusual and unexpected dichotomy that was first indicated by Alan Watts.) Christopher Hyatt's work is the closest technique to this model.

The author was, amongst many other things, a classical psychologist, a practitioner of Reichian therapy, and a 20-year student of the occult. From years of clinical experience he has distilled the essence of his experience in a most astute and shocking manner. In a fantastically penetrating, humorous and insightful fashion he has also distilled the essential factor in Zen meditative techniques. The result is a meditative system that is wholly unlike any other. Even the design of the book and the way it is presented suggests the purpose of the Great Work. As such it can be altogether recommended to those who have tried all other systems of meditation and found them wanting; their failure can be compensated for and overcome by the use of this extraordinary dynamic approach.

I recommend it enthusiastically and without any reservation whatsoever. In fact I am excited and exhilarated by its discovery.

It should prove to be the answer to the frustration felt by the thousands and more who have tried the other systems and failed. However, I do warn the reader, if you don't really want to change, don't take this book seriously.

Israel Regardie
March 11, 1982
SOMEWHERE HAVING FUN

ROLL AWAY THE STONE
New Falcon Publications, First Edition, 2017
An Introduction to Aleister Crowley's Essays
on the Psychology of Hashish

I

"O my Son, yester Eve came the Spirit upon me that I should eat the Grass of the Arabians," wrote Aleister Crowley pontifically (in *The Book of Wisdom or Folly*) concerning hashish around 1917-18 in New York City. "And by Virtue of the Bewitchment thereof beheld that which might be appointed for the Enlightenment of mine Eyes. Now then of this may I not speak, seeing that it involveth the Mystery of Transcending of Time, so that in One Hour of our Terrestrial Measure did I gather the harvest of an Aeon, and in Ten Lives I could not declare it."

Some years before the above was written, this English poet and mystic had produced a series of ten large magazine-like volumes with board covers entitled *The Equinox*. The intention was to publish a separate issue every Spring and Autumn for five years–making ten numbers in all. Openly published in them were his superbly written essays on the psychology of hashish. There were his earliest overt admissions to the occasional use of hashish as a psychedelic agent.

The first four issues of this periodical contained an important serial entitled *The Herb Dangerous*. The opening essay, *The Pharmacy of Hashish*, by an English chemist, E. Whineray, was a clinical and chemical analysis of *Cannabis Indica*, whose first cousin is marijuana, *Cannabis Sattiva*.

The second essay entitled *The Psychology of Hashish* was written by Oliver Haddo, one of the innumerable pseudonyms used by Aleister Crowley. It was succeeded in the third issue by *The Poem of Hashish*, written by Charles Baudelaire, and translated beautifully from the French by Crowley himself.

The final installment of the serial consisted of selections from a fantastic piece of writing by H. G. Ludlow entitled *The Hashish Eater*. Easily a rival to de Quincy's *Confessions of an Opium Eater*, Ludlow's book was published by Harpers (New York, 1857), and now being out of print should certainly be re-published in the near future. These are the four essays comprising the main body of this text.

Who was this Aleister Crowley?

An Englishman by birth, a great poet and essayist, he was also an intrepid explorer and a mountain climber of the Himalayas and other lofty peaks, and, above all these other talents, was a very great mystic. Despite these manifold claims to considerable fame, a sinister journalistic aura has gathered about him to obscure for all too long the vision of what the man was actually like. This obfuscation of the facts was partly due to his own vanity and lack of diplomacy, the other part to be laid at the door of the ignorance and vindictiveness of some journalists who preyed vulture-like on his least unconventional act. The tragic outcome, however, is that there are few people today who know what he really stood for. Some few may have heard the usual scandalous rumors that he used drugs, was profligate sexually, was wholly without morals, and for these reasons had been roundly condemned by both the British Press and by the Hearst publications in the United States. I can still remember from boyhood the full-page spreads in the magazine section of one of the yellow Sunday newspapers giving the most lurid and sensational accounts of some of his activities.

Insofar as Crowley was a mystic, he was known to the cultists of his day. Many of them considered him unequivocally evil and degenerate, though, despite this, some have not hesitated to steal much of his written material, using it altogether without acknowledgement. No one had a good word for him–save for an occasional reviewer of his verse, such as Gilbert K. Chesterton.

Much the same is true of many of the "metafizzlers" of today. I have read some of their recent literature condemning psychedelic drugs outright, as if these were a diabolical threat to their particular brand of mysticism. The most recent attack appeared in a Hollywood metaphysical monthly penned by a sincere enough writer who represents himself as a disciple of a stout ridiculous-looking Hindu "avatar", who, sworn to absolute silence, has not opened his mouth to speak for years, so it is said.

Instead–as if this were not speaking!–he uses a pointer and printed alphabet-board through which he communicates divine authoritative messages to a God-hungry world. His face and neck, however, look as though he has used his mouth rather well for purposes other than talking. This is the type and symbol of many of Crowley's critics.

Recent years have evolved a roster of new and eloquent voices to corroborate and to confirm many of Crowley's once outrageous views relative to the psychedelic agents: Aldous Huxley, Alan Watts, Timothy Leary and Richard Alpert–to name but a few among the more commonly known celebrities who in our day are directing attention to the dramatic fact that there is now a chemical door which gives promise to open to higher and mystical states of consciousness. This is what Crowley, amongst other things, had been trying to state more than half a century ago.

There is nothing radically new in their approach. But the one thing that is different is the laboratory development of a new chemical product which promises infinitely more reliability and effectiveness than, let us say, hashish, the drug that Crowley had once extolled in the absence of superior agents. He was not without awareness of the fact that hashish was an unpredictable drug, for he once wrote that the various preparation of *Cannabis Indica* are all alike in their action is so uncertain as to be not easily or surely standardized. It is not even a question of reasonable limits, he said; of two samples seemingly alike one may apparently degenerate fifty percent in strength within a few days. Some samples may be totally inert. It is this fact that has led to the total abandonment of the use of the drug in medicine. But, at the time he was writing, it was the best one he had been able to discover.

II

How did Crowley first make the discovery that drugs could stimulate or initiate the mystical state?

To begin with, it is certain that he had become familiar with the Grifford Lectures of William James, whose experimental frame of mind would have been wholly pleasing to the eager, intense young man just down from Cambridge. He must have read that wonderful passage that James had written:

> "Some years ago I myself made some observations on this aspect of nitrous oxide intoxication, and reported them in print. One conclusion was forced upon my mind at that time, and my impression of its truth has ever since remained unshaken. It is that our normal waking consciousness, rational consciousness, as we'll call it, is but one specific type of consciousness, whilst all about it, parted from it by the flimsiest of screens, there lie potential forms of consciousness entirely different. We may go through life without suspecting their existence; but apply the requisite stimulus, and at a touch they are there in all their completeness, definite types of mentality which probably somewhere have their field of application and adaptation..."

Not long after he came down from Cambridge in 1898, Crowley was introduced to membership in the Hermetic Order of the Golden Dawn, a nineteenth century secret society which taught an archaic system of ritual magic. This system, which served as the basis for his own organization which he founded a decade later, needs brief description at least, together with its Eastern counterpart–yoga. How he came to unite and correlate yoga and magic into a single exalted discipline to lead to the inner heights and depths, certainly had roots in ancient traditions, but to him nonetheless, was a stroke of individual genius.

The Golden Dawn was an occult organization formulated out of some British high masonic lodges in the year 1878. Authorization for its institution in England seems to have come from the continent, from alleged descendants of mediaeval Rosicrucian groups. It was thus a secret Rosicrucian body.

Its three chiefs, also high-grade Masons, believed, amongst other things, that women should not be disbarred from membership as they had been from Freemasonry. Artists, lawyers, physicians, actors, actresses, and humble men and women from all walks of life were included amongst its members. Many famous writers were also members–William Butler Yeats, Arthur Edward Waite, Algernon Blackwood, Arthur Machen, J. W. Brodie-Innes and a host of other luminaries of the literary world.

There were ceremonial grades and degrees not too dissimilar to those in the Masonic Order, the major difference being that certain occult teachings were transmitted to the aspirant during the ceremony. After he had successfully passed an examination that preceded advancement to successively higher grades, he was given further teachings and certain exercises to do. Naturally, Crowley sailed through these examinations and degrees with flying colors and at great speed. He was an intense and vigorous young man and poet. Since he had read widely and profoundly prior to joining the Order at the hoary age of 23 years, there was not much at first in the way of theory that the Order could surprise him with.

As an occult organization, The Golden Dawn maintained the strictest secrecy. Initially, its membership was selected with the utmost scrupulousness, an attitude which later was definitely relaxed. Its teachings and methods of instruction were guarded by penalties attached to the most awe-inspiring obligations in order to ensure that secrecy. Later, as changes were made in governance of the Order because of the death of one chief and the resignation of another, dictatorial powers were assumed by McGregor Mathers who was a Qabalist of some distinction. He was the translator of three mediaeval magical texts: *The Greater Key of King Solomon, The Kabbalah Unveiled* (which consisted of certain portions for Knorr von Rosenroth's Latin rendition of the *Zohar*, prefixed by a lengthy introduction of some erudition), and *The Book of the Sacred Magic of Abramelin in Mage*.

With the passage of time, a revolt broke out amongst the rank and file of the Order's membership, presumably because of the irrational dictator-like attitudes of Mathers. Of course, there was the usual bickering, slander, and a lot of scandal, in which, unfortunately Crowley came to play a prominent part.

Internal dissension continued for some years until it came to a blistering head with one group of members expelling its own Chief. Mathers retained a small handful of loyal adherents.

Yeats belonged to one of the dissident groups, Arthur E. Waite, whom Kenneth Rexroth has referred to amusingly as "a scholar" formed another faction which he named the Reconstructed-Rosicrucian Order. It became stultified, burdened as it was by the massive weight of Waite's pompous jargon and ponderous literary style. Other groups were reorganized in various parts of Great Britain, all of them persisting in the prime work of the Order–to teach magical procedures as the Way to the Light.

In a few words, Magic is the same for a primitive psychological system. Its goal was illumination, being "brought to the Light." The transcendental experience to be reached by means of ritual and other technical procedures was at the heart of the system, which can hardly be guessed at by the uninformed layman, but which some psychologists, including Carl G. Jung (and who form, what Abraham Maslow call the Third School) have been profoundly impressed with.

Some of the more ancient schools of initiation must have employed drugs as one kind or another in a sacramental manner. What specific products they actually did use is not at all clear. Henbane, belladonna, hashish, opium and the solanaceaes have all been suspected. The modern school, headed by Mathers in the last quarter of the 19th century, frowned upon all such methods, preferring the classical secret techniques of mind and spiritual training.

Willis W. Harman, in a sensitively written essay "The Issue of the Consciousness-Expanding Drugs" (*Main Currents*, Vol. 20, No.1, 1963) asserted that down through the ages of recorded history, various groups within the several religious traditions alike have insisted that man has far vaster potentiality for knowledge, and hence power over his fate, then he ordinarily dreams of as possible. These included the ancient Gnostics to the modern Theosophists, including also the Hindu, Buddhist, Moslem and Christian religions. They have always claimed that it is possible to *know*–in a way that is completely different from the mere accumulation of facts–to realize man's essential nature and his true relationship to the creative force behind or within the universe. There, wrote Harman, his fulfillment lies–that is, what it is he values most highly when the meaning of life is clearly seen. For this particular species of knowledge, men have followed religious teachers of every shade and opinion, and joined secret societies. They have willingly submitted to the travail of elaborate initiation procedures and trained for years in different yoga and meditation techniques. They have practiced fasting, flagellation and all kinds of austerity. Among them all, the experience of *gnosis*, of direct perception and knowledge, has been most highly prized of all human experiences and attainments.

Magic then, being a primitive psychological technique that in recent times was taught and practiced within the Golden Dawn, it is evident that Crowley had been fully exposed to it once he became a member. A few years after such initiation, when he had become proficient as a practicing student, he wrote an essay entitled *The Initiated Interpretation of Ceremonial Magic*, large parts of which need to be quoted here if only as a semantic device to define my terms.

As a prelude, I must state that at that time he was not familiar with psychoanalysis. Nothing in that field had yet been translated into English. Thus he was not acquainted with many of our now commonplace and popular mental constructs–such as the Unconscious, superego, libido, psycho-dynamics, and so forth. Instead, since he had studied some little neurology, he attempted to explain the results of Magic and Yoga in terms of cerebral physiology as he understood it, and adapted it to the exigencies of his thesis.

Though the essay is rather long, it is worthy of extensive quotation to show his rationalistic approach to these difficult and complex psycho-spiritual problems.

"It is loftily amusing to the student of magical literature who is not quite a fool–and rare is such a combination!–to note the criticism directed by the Philistine against the citadel of his science...I am not concerned to deny the objective reality of all 'magical' phenomena; if they are illusions, they are at least as real as many unquestioned facts of daily life; and , if we follow Herbert Spencer, they are at least evidence of some *cause*.

"Now this fact is our base. What is the cause of my illusion of seeing a spirit in the triangle of Art?

"Every smatterer, every expert in psychology, will answer: 'That cause lies in your brain.'

"English children are taught (*pace* the Education Act) that the Universe lies in Infinite Space; Hindu children, in the Akasa, which is the same thing.

"Those Europeans who go a little deeper learn from Fichte, that the phenomenal Universe is the Creation of the Ego; Hindus, or Europeans studying under Hindu Gurus, are told that by Akasa is meant the Chit-akasa. The Chit-akasa is situated in the 'Third Eye,' i.e., in the brain. By assuming higher dimensions of space, we can assimilate this fact to Realism; but we have no need to take so much trouble.

"This being true for the ordinary Universe, that all sense-impressions are dependent on changes in the 'brain', we must include illusions, which are after all sense-impressions as much as 'realities' are, in the class of phenomena dependent on brain-changes.

"Magical phenomena, however, come under a special sub-class, since they are willed, and their cause is the series of 'real' phenomena called the operations of Ceremonial Magic.

These consist of:

(1) Sight.
　　The circle, square, triangle, vessels, lamps, robes, implements, etc.
(2) Sound.
　　The invocation.
(3) Smell.
　　The perfumes.
(4) Taste.
　　The sacraments.
(5) Touch.
　　As under (1).
(6) Mind.
　　The combination of all these and reflections on their significance.

"These unusual impressions (1-5) produce unusual brain changes; hence their summary (6) is of unusual kind. Its projection back into the apparently phenomenal world is therefore unusual.

"Herein then consists the reality of the operations and effects of ceremonial magic, and I conceive that the apology is ample, so far as the 'effects' refer only to those phenomena which appear to the magician himself, the appearance of the spirit, his conversation, possible shocks from imprudence, and so on, even to ecstasy on the one hand, and death or madness on the other...

"And this is a purely materialistic rational statement; it is independent of any objective hierarchy at all. Philosophy has nothing to say; and Science can only suspend judgement, pending a proper and methodical investigation of the facts alleged...Our Ceremonial Magic finds down, then, to a series of minute, though of course, empirical, psychological experiments, and who so will carry them through intelligently need not fear the results..."

Magical principles, similar to those just described, are being spontaneously applied at "happenings' that one occasionally hears of. These occur amongst some of the '"hippy" and "swinger" exponents of the contemporary psychedelic movement. For example, from one description recently recounted, the following picture can be reconstructed:

(1) Sight.
Colors, lights, swiftly flashing in kaleidoscopic movement, influencing the brain through the optic nerve.

(2) Sound.
The noisiest kind of music, popular or classical, which blasts the mind almost into oblivion or insensibility.

(3) Smell.
Marihuana is occasionally being used to heighten nervous system activity. Its peculiar, characteristic odor is stimulating for some people.

(4) Taste.
Again, both alcohol (in moderate usage) and marihuana are used for gustatory stimulation.

(5) Touch.
In a few instances, one hears of "orgies" and wife-swapping in the above context. The feel of bodies, warm skin, genitals, coitus, heighten the tactile experience.

(6) Mind.
All of these–and perhaps their summation in the "peak" experience..

A large number of changes may be wrung upon these simple basic themes.

III

What was really important, however, about this whole Order theme was his confrontation with two men who were members of the higher, so-called Adept grades. They were destined to play an enormous role in his own subsequent spiritual development. One of these was George Cecil Jones, a chemist and metallurgist, who remained in the closest contact with Crowley for many long years. He was friend, counsellor and advisor.

The other was Allan Bennett, of no consistent vocation. It has been said that he was an electrical engineer, a keen student of Eastern religions and philosophy–and a financially handicapped man. His enfeebled economic status was due, in part anyway, to his suffering from chronic bronchial asthma which had played havoc with his health and efficiency. It apparently prevented him from successfully exploiting his talents in any rewarding manner.

Because he was practically "down and out" when Crowley first met him, Allan was invited to share Crowley's apartment for an indefinite period of time. Money at that time presented no problem to Crowley, he having inherited a considerable sum. Allan thus became Crowley's guest, and perhaps for the first time in many years was well-housed, well-fed and well-clothed.

Inasmuch as Allan was an advanced adept of the Golden Dawn, his part of the *quid pro quo* was to teach Crowley whatever he knew of the magical arts. This task he accepted, and performed extremely well. Crowley proved to be an apt pupil, and Allan knew what he was doing. Together they accomplished a great deal, and the intellectual traces of this relationship remained with Crowley all his life.

Subsequently, Allan gave up the entire Golden Dawn methodology–and, with Crowley's financial and other kinds of aid, left England for the Far East, his severe and chronic asthma playing a decisive role. There, in a far warmer and more satisfactory climate, he was relieved of much of his respiratory difficulty. In fact, it was while he was in Ceylon that he became converted to Buddhism, and in so doing fulfilled a lifelong dream. Under the new sacramental name of Bhikkhu Ananda Metteya, he played an important and efficient role in helping to bring Thera Vada Buddhism to the Western World. Crowley's utilization of the Buddhist skandhas as an analytical schema in *The Psychology of Hashish* can be traced directly to Allan.

What is most significant about this close association of the two men, however, is this fundamental fact. While living in Crowley's flat in London for about a year and a half, Allan was obliged to use many different drugs to obtain even temporary relief from his severe asthamatic paroxysm. The cold, damp and foggy English weather played havoc with his wheezy respiratory system. Some drugs seemed to work fairly well at first; others were grossly ineffectual. But even when a few did work, he had to use such enormous quantities that he became poisoned by them. For varying periods of time, he would be laid low and was lethargic, sleepy and inert.

However, in addition to the sought-after relief from the bronchial spasms, he came to discover that some of the medications he employed were psychedelics as we would now term them. They expanded the horizons of the mind, and dissolved the boundaries of the ego, occasionally inducing ineffable states of mystic consciousness with which he was already familiar as a result of his meditative and devotional exercises.

Thus intrigued, he became a concentrated and profound student of pharmacology as it existed at that time, reading far and wide, and most intelligently too. He experimented with whatever drugs he could lay hands on. The immediate goal was to find that one magical drug which would open door to these higher states.

This was the basis thesis. And it was this thesis that Crowley inherited from Allan. It was adopted wholly and joyfully. Crowley too came to study pharmacology. He discussed the problem with many physicians, physiologists and neurologists, and experimented even more enthusiastically and extensively than had his guru, Allan Bennett.

(As an aside, it should be mentioned as a most curious phenomenon, that Crowley also came to develop bronchial asthma after several years had elapsed. Several of his intimate friends and later disciples also suffered from asthma.)

Meanwhile, he had the wanderlust. The world was his oyster. Having inherited a considerable fortune from his relatives connected with the brewing industry in the south of England, his wish to travel was made easy. He hiked, explored, climbed mountains in Scotland, Switzerland, Mexico, and eventually India–attempted to emulate many of the exotic feats of another of his life-long idols, Sir Richard Burton. He walked across that part of the Sahara Desert adjoining Algeria and Tunisia, mingling freely with the Arabs whose masculinity and virility he came to admire. There also he met sheikhs of innumerable types and levels of importance, discovering that some of them were familiar with the use of drugs that exalted and expanded consciousness. He learned from them, and learned well. It is quite certain that under their tutelage, he learned a lot more than merely homosexual practices. Through the administration of these exotic drugs, including hashish of course, he experienced a wide variety of higher states of consciousness, about which he has written more illuminatingly than almost anyone else I know.

During a protracted visit to Ceylon, where he had gone to visit Allan Bennett, he practiced Yoga and studied oriental philosophies with his characteristic vigor and enthusiasm. On two separate occasions in the first five years of this century, he climbed some of the highest peaks of the Himalayas, and almost made it–but not quite. However, one of the results of these expeditions was that he did enter the small mountain kingdoms of Nepal and Sikhim adjacent to Tibet, where he acquired considerable practical knowledge of Buddhist and lamaistic Tantric methods. The residue is palpable in his earliest technical writings.

So far as Yoga is concerned, one of the most authoritative of the ancient texts, Patanjali's Yoga aphorisms, defines Yoga as "the hindering of the modifications of the thinking principle." Briefly, then, it is that psychological process which has concentration as its goal. That this achievement is considered to be the prime necessity or prerequisite to the attainment of spiritual experience, or Samadi as it is called, is implicit in all the principal Eastern mystical writings. Having practised this art for many years and having become a master, as it were, of concentration and meditation, Crowley has written about this subject with wit, with clarity, and with an authoritative simplicity which is nowhere else to be found. One little book entitled *Part I of Book IV* is a gem of clarity and wisdom. In several of the *Equinox* publications are to be found a dozen or more classics of instruction in the various aspects of Yoga posture, breathing, concentration and so forth–all beautifully written and free of superfluity.

I should interpolate at this point that because of his effervescing sense of humor, which bubbled all over the place and penetrated almost everything he wrote, some readers and many critics saw merely a funny man. It never occurred to most of them that involved in his humor was a deadly serious purpose. It was a literary and psychological technique employed for a number of well-defined ends. Nor merely to separate the wheat from the chaff, but mainly to separate the sheep from the goats. Thus it was used to test the reader. If the latter could not take this debunking and still clamoured for the old veneer of verbiage and superstition, this was not the kind of person to be encouraged in the Great Work. Or, if he were deceived by the humor into believing that there was nothing else present, Crowley thought that here was a fanatic who should be altogether discouraged from attempting this work. He felt that when the passage became rough, or when the external and internal pressures increased, as they were bound to do, such a person would succumb to neurotic illness, or worse. Crowley wanted none of these.

In a rather later work entitled Eight Lectures on Yoga, which is rich in commonsense, subtle humor, and an uncomplicated exposition of its deepest meanings, we find the following:

"(1) There is more nonsense talked about and written about Yoga than about anything else in the world. Most of this nonsense, which is fostered by charlatans, is based upon the idea that there is something mysterious and Oriental about it. There isn't. Do not look to me for obelisks and odalesques, Rahat Loucoum, bul-buls, or any other tinsel imagery of the Yoga mongers. I am neat but not gaudy. There is nothing mysterious or Oriental about anything, as everybody knows who has spent a little time intelligently in the continents of Asia and Africa...

"(2) All phenomena of which we are aware take place in our own minds, and therefore the only thing we have to look at is the mind: which is a more constant quantity over all the species of humanity than is generally supposed...

"(3) We must then begin the study of Yoga by looking at the meaning of the word. It means Union, from the same Sanskirt root as the Greek word Zeugma, the Latin word Jugum, and the English work yoke. (Yeaung - to join)...

"(4) Yoga means Union.

"In what sense are we to consider this? How is the word Yoga to imply a system of religious training that the word Religion is really identifiable with Yoga. It means a binding together.

"(5) Yoga means Union.

"What are the elements which are united or to be united when this word is used in its common sense of a practice widely spread in Hindustan whose object is the emancipation of the individual who studies and practices it from the less pleasing features of his life on this planet?

"In the mind of a pious person, the inferiority complex which accounts for his piety compels him to interpret this emancipation as union with the gaseous vertebrate whom he has invented and called God. On the cloudy vapour of his fears, his imagination has thrown a vast distorted shadow of himself, and he is duly terrified...It is because of his overwhelming miasma of fear that the whole subject of Yoga has become obscure. A perfectly simple problem has been complicated by the most abject ethical and superstitious nonsense. Yet all the time the truth is patent in the word itself...

"It may seem to some of you that these explanations have rather knocked the bottom out of Yoga; that I have reduced it to the category of common things. That was my object. There is no sense in being frightened of Yoga, awed by Yoga, muddled or mystified by Yoga, or enthusiastic over Yoga...

"On the *terrasse* of the Cafe des Deux Magots it was once necessary to proclaim the entire doctrine of Yoga in the fewest possible words 'with a shout, and with the voice of the archangel and with the Trump of God.' St. Paul's First Epistle to the Thessalonians, the Fourth Chapter and the sixteenth verse. I did so.

"Sit still. Stop thinking. Shut up. Get Out!"

This is Crowley at his rationalistic best. It is to be more than favourable compared with Leary's mantram "Turn on, tune in, drop out!" Basically, the difference between Leary and Crowley is that the latter made a special plea for discipline and training in the meditative arts as a major means of exploring the inner world of mind and spirit. In fact, this is the main point of these four essays on hashish. As a chemical tool to be harnessed to the employment of trained concentration and meditation, lysergic acid has much to be said for it. Crowley's contention was that we should thus expect far better results with its use than if the tool of meditation alone was used, and vice versa.

IV

It was about ten years after he had first been initiated into the Hermetic Order of the Golden Dawn, that Crowley finally came to a standstill in England to form his own training organization. Those were ten long, significant and fruitful years spent in wandering over the face of the earth, experimenting with every known method of inducing the highest mystical states. Many of the traditional contents of the Golden Dawn became incorporated into the structure of his own order, the A∴A∴ Yet, in many ways, the latter differed immeasurably from its predecessor. Principally, the major difference rested in his unification of Yoga and Magic into a single system having as its goal the attainment of Light.

Each of his travels had yielded a grain of some technique or inner discipline that could be utilized as a minute segment in the vast mosaic or panorama of methods and scientific approach. Some little view of this wide vista can be perceived in his essay The Psychology of Hashish. Clearly, it is not the work of a narrow-minded crackpot or fanatic. Really to appreciate the genius of this man, one should have become familiar with the technical instructions that he has written on all phases of the two ancient systems he had worked with. It must be accepted as factual that in each one, he had achieved the summit. This is evidenced by the content and context of the so-called official instructions of his Order, as well as by the following, which is particularly apt today when so many inexperienced youngsters are getting their "kicks' from the psychedelic drugs:

"Just so one's first dazzled delight in a new landscape turns, as one continues to gaze, to the appreciation of exquisite details of the view. At first they were blurred by the blinding rush of general beauty; they emerge one by one as the shock subsides, and passionate rapture yields to intelligent interest.

"In the same way the Adept almost always begins by torrential lyrics panting out mystical extravagances about 'ineffable love,' 'unimaginable bliss,' (This corresponds to the emotional and metaphysical fog which is the characteristic of the emergence of thought from homogeneity. The clear and concise differentiation of ideas marks the adult mind.) He usually loses his sense of proportion, of humour, of reality, and of sound judgement. His ego is often inflated to the bursting point, till he would be abjectly ridiculous if he were not so pitifully dangerous to himself and others. He also tends to take his new-found truths of illumination for the entire body of truth, and insists that they must be as valid and vital for men as they happen to be for himself."

It will have to be assumed that the general reader is by and large unfamiliar with what Crowley strove for. To remedy this defect, let us assume you were a student of mysticism and had applied to him as a so-called authority for training in the methods of the Great Work. This is an archaic term referring to the self discipline leading to enlightenment. The first responsibility set for the beginner was to do some reading from a preliminary list of authoritative literature given to him for study. When he had completed this mass of reading in some three months, he could apply for a written examination of the study material. The prime intention here was only to ensure that he had, at the very least, acquired as intellectual familiarity with basic classical material.

In the event that the student showed promise, and was theoretically familiar with, let us say, William James' *Varieties of*

Religious Experience and other similar analyses of and descriptions of mystical and transcendental states of consciousness, Crowley *might* recommend the use of hashish. At the time when Crowley wrote his books, such drugs were procurable without a prescription, at any chemist or pharmacy without breaking the established laws of England.

The purpose of this hashish-session was simply to provide the student with a fore-taste or some adumbration of the mystical experience towards which he was focusing all his energies. It was *never* the intention of Crowley at any time to use drugs as a substitute for the body-mind-discipline which he insisted on beyond all other things. This was the furthest notion from his mind. We must take him seriously when he asserted.

"I have no use for hashish save as a preliminary demonstration that there exists another world attainable–somehow. *Possibly if pharmacists were to concentrate their efforts upon producing a standard drug...we might find a valuable and harmless adjuvant to the process which I have optimistically names Scientific Illuminism."* (Italics are mine.)

I want to emphasize unequivocally that Crowley has asserted not once but a thousand times that the discipline itself was far more important than any other particular result or attainment. His thesis was that in training a concert pianist for example, one concentrations on drills, scales and exercises until enough manual dexterity and self-discipline has been developed to play Beethoven's *Emperor Concerto*. One does not start with the latter. It is in this area that he differs seriously from most of our contemporaries.

However, since human nature is human nature after all, and since people do tend to become discouraged and, from there, give up the struggle for enlightenment, Crowley contended that if they could be given some inkling of what the ineffable experience could be like, perhaps then they would be willing to overcome their own inertia and despondency–and work. It was the carrot to be waved in front of the donkey's nose. But waved only long enough to get the donkey started!

"Let it not be imagined," he wrote, "that I devised these thoughts from pure sloth or weariness. But with the mystical means then at my disposal, I required a period of days or weeks to obtain any Result...If only, therefore, I could reduce the necessary period to a few hours...My present appeal is to recognized physiologists and psychologists to increase the number and accuracy of their researches on the introspective lines which I have laid down above, possibly with further aid from the pharmacist.

"Once the pure physio-psychological action is determined, I shall then ask their further attention to the special results of combining the drug with the mystic process–always involving training observation–and from that moment the future of Scientific Illuminism will be assured." (Italics mine.)

Well, what he did hope for has been partly fulfilled. The chemists did produce lysergic acid in 1938, though some of its first psychic sequelae were not observed until 1945. Sad to say, that though Crowley lived to 1947, he was never aware of the fact that lysergic acid had been created and was really the drug of choice, the ideal chemical he had yearned for as the experimental aid to the magico-mystical system he had developed.

One of Timothy Leary's former associates, Frank Ferguson, who gave up graduate work in anthropology to further the progress of a now defunct organization devoted to disseminating information about lysergic acid, once explained that Eastern mystics were able to control their nervous systems after some twenty to thirty years of study and self-discipline. He hastened to add, presumptuously I think, that, with the aid of the hallucinogens, these yogic skills might be taught in a matter of a few weeks. It was his opinion that the long and arduous traditional discipline of the yogis were nowadays not required for what Leary has described as "drug-induced satori." This promise, naturally, is most appealing to all of us; *satori* without tears! Another writer in *The Harvard Review* commented that people who have worked with lysergic acid have hoped to find a quick and easy way to reach the inner goals that, in the past, have only been attained by those who were willing to undergo the pain and work associated with the ancient disciplines.

This was far indeed from Aleister Crowley's basic premise. As a counter to this, as though in anticipation of such abuse of oversimplification, he wrote:

> "I could persuade other people that mysticism was not all folly without insisting on their devoting a lifetime to studying under me; and if only I could convince a few competent observers–in such a matter I distrust even myself–Science would be bound to follow and to investigate, clear up the matter once for all, and, as I believed, and believe, arm itself with a new weapon ten thousand times more potent than the balance and the microscope."

His fundamental premise was stated over and over again, in a hundred different ways. It was *never* that the drug experience per se could possible replace the basic mental and spiritual discipline that he stood for, and which all previous occult teachers insisted upon. In fact, he was relatively certain that whatever the drug experience did evoke would soon be forgotten to become a cold, gray, vague memory.

"As one would expect, such forms leave little impress upon the memory. Yet they are seductive enough, and I am afraid that the very great majority of mystics live all their lives wandering about in this vain world of shadows and of shells...What vain folly (of all true hope forlorn!) to seek in drugs, in drink, in the pistol or the cord, the paradise they have forfeited by a moment's weakness or a moment's wavering..."

What was required beyond all other things was endurance and persistency–the discipline of the body-mind system, in all the technical phases of the Work itself, to provide the basic necessary tools through which the mystical state would be reinstated, re-experienced, and explored.

Huston Smith, who wrote an essay in the LSD book edited by David Solomon, believes similarly to Crowley. He wrote:

> "The case of Zen is especially pertinent here, for it pivots on an enlightened experience–*satori* or *kensho*–which some (but not all) Zennists say resembles LSD. Alike or different, the point is that Zen recognizes that unless the experience is joined to discipline, it will come to naught."

And then Smith proceeds to add, what is most significant to this thesis, that"

> "Even the Buddha had to sit...Without *jo riki*, the particular power developed through *zazen* (seated meditation), the vision of oneness attained in enlightenment...in time becomes clouded and eventually fades into a pleasant memory instead of remaining an omnipresent reality shaping our daily life... To be able to live in accordance with what the Mind's eye has revealed through *Satori* requires, like the purification of character and the development of personality, a ripening period of *zazen*."

Crowley indicated, though, that there might be occasions, even when one had acquired supreme skill in meditation, when an additional fillip or stimulus provided by the judicious and temperate use of hashish would enable one to surmount the sterility and grimness of the long-protracted discipline, to soar exaltedly above the armour restriction of the ego-function into the ineffable. The opening of his own hashish essay deals with this very problem.

> "I was also aware of the prime agony of meditation, the 'dryness' (as Molinos calls it) which hardens and sterilizes the soul.

"The very practice which should flood it with light leads only to a darkness more terrible than death, a despair and disgust which only too often lead to abandonment, when in truth they should encourage, for that–as the oracles affirm–it is the darkness before the dawn.

"Meditation therefore annoyed me," he commented wryly, "as tightening and constricting the soul. I began to ask if the 'dryness' was an essential part of the process. If by some means I could shake its catafalque of Mind, might not the Infinite Divine Spirit leap unfettered to the Light?"

And then he asks eloquently, for never let it be forgotten this man was a master of meditation: "Who shall roll away the stone?"

To answer his own question, he formulated the hypothesis: "Perhaps hashish is the drug which 'loosens the girders of the soul,' but in itself neither good nore bad...Well, then, let me see whether by first exalting myself mystically and continuing my invocations while the drug dissolves the matrix of the diamond Soul, that diamond might not manifest limpid and sparkling, a radiance 'not of the Sun, nor of the Moon, nor of the Stars';..."

V

What is meant by the mystical experience is capable of a variety of explanations. We can use the idiom of modern psychological language, advancing the notion that the drug somehow attenuates the character armor or the mental defense mechanisms which cramp and stricture the psyche.

This attenuation would permit the emergence from the Unconscious of feelings, emotions, energy and other psychic contents, long buried, or which never yet have seen the light of day. Their emergence would thus expand the limited horizons of consciousness and permit the experience of oceanic or nirvanic feelings. The attack on the ego functions is a deliberate controlled matter when meditation and concentration exercises are employed–as in Yoga and Zen–but, of course, more fortuitous when a psychedelic drug is employed. A new school of psychologists is developing currently. They regard the mystical experience as a healthy development in the onward growth of the psyche. They do not consider this phenomenon outside of their psychological field, as did nineteenth century science. Since it is a piece of naturalistic human behavior, it is regarded as well within their scientific purview, rather than as belonging to the field of religion. Instead of the familiar phrase the "religious" or "mystical" experience, they have coined a new phase, the "peak" experience to refer to the same inner phenomenon. They are inclined to view its occurrence as a good deal more common than was previously supposed, and that there is a spontaneity in this frequency. More often than not, in non-religious people such as poets and artists, it is not evoked or precipitated by the use of prayer, devotion and other religious techniques.

"There is no difference in principle between sharpening perception with an external instrument, such as a microscope," wrote Alan Watts, "and sharpening it with an internal instrument, such as one of these three drugs. If they are an affront to the dignity of the eye and the telephone to the dignity of the ear..."

A neurological explanation is also possible, and, all other things being equal, is just as valid. For example, there is one provided by Leary:

"The facts of the neurological capacities of the human being are simply astronomical. We possess, each of us, around 10 billion brain cells. This is several times the number of human beings in the world. Any one brain cell can be in relationship with as many as 25,000 others. The number of possible associations is of the order of 10 billion to the twenty-five-thousandth power, a quantity larger than the number of atoms in the universe. This electrical-chemical network, inconceivable in its complexity, is the anatomical structure of consciousness...

"How can we explain this extraordinary discrepancy between the potentials of the cortical computer and the poverty of the programs we impose on it? There is little known about the function of the brain and about the learning processes by means of which the brain's enormous potential is limited and contracted. The term which seems most adequate to describe the process is imprinting.

"What is imprinting?...it is 'very rapid learning that takes place in some animals...at a certain early stage of development.'

"Another awesome aspect of the imprinting process is its unpredictable and accidental quality. Because Conrad Lorentz happened to be present at the right moment, the goslings 'imprinted' him as the protective, maternal object. In another experiment, young birds were presented with a Ping-Pong ball at the critical moment and spent their remaining life pursuing and making love to the plastic globes. This experiment is both amusing and frightening. It reminds us that each of us sees the world through perceptual structures (biochemical-neurological) which were laid down accidently in our earliest moments. It raises the uneasy suspicion that, in spite of our vaunted rationality and conditioned certainty, we may be simply chasing the particular Ping-Pong balls which, at those sensitive shutter moments, had been imprinted on our cortical film...

"Certain alkaloid molecules possess the power of dramatically suspending the familiar, learned structure aspects of the nervous system; Consciousness is suddenly released from its conditioned patterning and flung into a flashing loom of unlearned imagery. However heatedly scientists may disagree about the value and social meaning of the psychedelic drugs, there is one point upon which they concur; the drugs do propel awareness into an eerie, novel landscape in which everything seems possible and nothing remains fixed...The psychedelic drugs may not only suspend old imprinted patterns, they may also provide the possibility of the 'death-rebirth' experience which is so often reported during psychedelic moments. Re-imprinting means that during the psychedelic session the subject's nervous system is in a state of disorganized flux closely analogous to that of infancy. The planned, voluntary release of fixed perceptual patterns and the temporary opening up of fluid, boundaryless awareness suggests the hope of controlled, self-controlling re-imprinting."

We can proceed further to the religious concept, that the mystical experience represents Union with God. Crowley could be theistic as with Vedanta, or non-theistic as with Thera-Vada Buddhism, as he chose, depending on the circumstances. But whichever philosophical stance he adopted, it presented no problem to him as a vehicle to interpret life experiences, whether mystical or secular. In fact, more often than not, he adopted the non-theistic position as being more utilitarian. This is expressed rather well in the following excerpt from his *Gospel According to St. Bernard Shaw*.

> "The mystic attainment may be defined as the Union of the Soul with God, or as the realization of itself, or–there are fifty phrases for the same experience. The same, for whether you are a Christian or a Buddhist, a Theist or (as I am myself, thank God!) an Atheist, the attainment of this one state is as open to you as is nightmare, or madness, or intoxication. Religious folk have buried this fact under mountains of dogma; but the study of comparative religion has made it clear. One has merely to print parallel passages from the mystics of all ages and religions to see that they were talking of the same things; one gets even verbal identities, such as the 'That Tao which is Tao is not Tao' of the Chinese, the 'Not That, Not That' of the Hindu, the 'Head which is above all Heads, the Head which is not a Head' of the Qabalist, the 'God is Nothing' of the Christians, and the 'That is not which is' of a modern atheistic or pantheistic mystic."

He could adopt yet other points of view which are as valid as the above. For instance, the following account is extrapolated from an early diary dated perhaps about 1909:

> "When therefore I had made ready the chamber, so that all was dark, save for the Lamp upon the Altar, I began as recorded

above, to inflame myself in praying, calling upon the Lord; and I burned in the Lamp that Pantacle which I had made of Him, renouncing the Images, that Himself might arise in me.

"And the Chamber was filled with that wondrous glow of ultraviolet light self-luminous without a source, that hath no counterpart in Nature unless it be in that Dawn of the North' The subtly, easily, simply, imperceptibly sliding, I passed away into nothing. And I was wrapped in the black brilliance of my Lord, that interpenetrated me in every part, fusing its light with my darkness, and leaving there no darkness, but pure light.

"Also I beheld my Lord in a figure and I felt the interior trembling kindle itself into a Kiss–and I perceived the true Sacraments–and I beheld in one moment all the mystic visions in one; and the Holy Graal appeared unto me, and many other inexpressible things were known to me.

"Also, I was given to enjoy the subtle presence of my Lord interiorly during the whole of this twelfth day.

"Then I besought the Lord that He would take me into His presence eternally even now.

"But he withdrew Himself, for that I must do that which I was sent hither to do...And the Light and the Perfume do certainly yet remain with me in the little Chamber, and I know that my Redeemer liveth, and that He shall stand at the latter day upon the earth...

"The clock of the Senate strikes; and my ears are ravished with its mysterious melody. It is the infinite interior movement of things, secured by the co-extension of their sum with the all, that transcends the deadly opposites; change which implies decay, stability which spells monotony.

"I understand all the Psalms of Benediction; there is spontaneous praise, a fountain in my heart. The authors of the Psalms must have known something of this Illumination when they wrote them...My soul is singing...My soul is singing!"

In attempting to make the above paean rational even to a mild degree, we could fall back on Science and Buddhism, an essay which he wrote about 1903, not too long after he had experienced his first Dhyana following intense Yoga practice. in this essay, he wrote:

"Suppose, however, a dream so vivid that the whole waking man is abased before its memory, that this consciousness of it appears a thousand times more real than that of the things about him; suppose that his whole life is moulded to fit the new facts thus revealed to him; that he would cheerfully renounce years of normal life to obtain minutes of that dream life; that his time sense is uprooted as never before, and that these influences are permanent. Then you will say, delirium tremens do not occur in the healthy. As for the suggestion of auto-hypnosis, the memory of the 'dream' is a sufficient reply. However this may be, the simple fact of the superior apparent reality–a conviction unshakable, *inépuisable* (for the English has no word) is a sufficient test. And if we condescend to argue, it is for pleasure, and aside from the vital fact; a skirmish, and not a pitched battle.

"The 'dream' I have described is the state called Dhyana by the Hindus and Buddhists. The method of attaining it is sane, healthy, and scientific...It is simple. The mind is compelled to fix its attention on a single thought; while the controlling power is exercised and a profound watchfulness kept up lest the thought should for a moment stray."

Or, he could avoid any one of the above postures with the utmost ease, or employ a more sceptical philosophical position, as indicated, for example, in his earliest book on Yoga, *Part I of Book IV:*

"In the course of our concentration *we noticed that the contents of the mind at any moment consisted of two things, and no more; the Object, variable, and the Subject, invariable, or apparently so. By success in Dharana the object has been made as invariable as the subject.*

"Now the result of this is that the two become one. This phenomenon usually comes as a tremendous shock. It is indescribable even by the master of language; and it is therefore not surprising that semi-educated stutterers wallow in oceans of gush.

"All the poetic faculties and all the emotional faculties are thrown into a sort of ecstasy by an occurrence which overthrows the mind, and makes the rest of life seem absolutely worthless in comparison...*Even when one has become accustomed to Dhyana by contrast repetition, no words seem adequate...The most important factor in Dhyana is, however, the annihilation of the Ego.* Our conception of the universe must be completely overturned if we are to admit this as valid; and it is time that we considered what is really happening...*The man who experienced any of the more intense forms of Dhyana is thus liberated. The Universe is thus destroyed for him, and he for it. His will can therefore go on its way unhampered...*A most astounding phenomenon has happened to us; we have had an experience which makes love, fame, rank, ambition, wealth, look like thirty cents; and we begin to wonder passionately, 'What is truth?' The Universe has tumbled about our ears like a house of cards and we have tumbled too. Yet this ruin is like the opening of the Gates of Heaven!"

In *A History of Zen Buddhism* by Heinrich Dumoulin, S. J., there is an account of the "Great Dying" which, in its own nontheistic way, would have been altogether accepted by Crowley, since it corresponded to one of his own mystical experiences during the walk across the Southern Border of China, near Vietnam, in the year 1906:

"If you wish to attain the true Nonego," says a monk Hakuin in that history, "you must release your hold over the abyss. If thereafter you revive you will come upon the true ego of the four virtues. What does it mean to release one's hold over the abyss? A man went astray and arrived at a spot which had never been trodden by the foot of man. Before him there yawned a bottomless chasm. His feet stood on the slippery moss of a rock and no secure foothold appeared around him. The vine which he grasped with his left hand and the tendril which he held with his right hand could offer him little help. His life hung as by a single thread. Were he to release both hands at once, his dry bones would come to nought.

"Thus it is with the Zen disciple. By pursuing a single *Koan* he comes to a point where his mind is as if dead and his will as if extinguished. This state is like a wide void over a deep chasm and no hold remains for hand or foot. All thoughts vanish and in his bosom burns hot anxiety. But then suddenly it occurs that with the *koan* both body and mind break. This is the instance when the hands are released over the abyss. In this sudden upsurge it is as if one drinks water and knows for oneself heat and cold. Great joy wells up. This is called rebirth (in the Pure Land). This is termed seeing into one's nature. Everything depends on pushing forward and not doubting that with the help of this concentration one will eventually penetrate to the ground of one's own nature.

In *The Psychology of Hashish*, reprinted herewith, Crowley had much more to say concerning the fundamental criteria of the mystical experience, which is worth quoting:

"It may be useful here to distinguish once and for all between false and real mystical phenomena; for in the previous sections we have spoken of both without distinction. In the 'astral visions' the consciousness is hardly disturbed; in magical evocations it is intensely exalted; but it is still bound by its original conditions. The Ego is still opposed to the non-Ego, time is, if altered in rate, still there; so, too, in Space, the sort of Space we are all conscious of. Again, the phenomena observed follow the usual laws of growth and decay.

"But all true mystical phenomena contradict these conditions.

"In the first place, the Ego and non-Ego unite explosively, their product having none of the qualities of either. It is precisely such a phenomenon as the direct combination of Hydrogen and Chlorine. The first thing observed is the flash; in our analogy, the ecstasy or ananda (bliss) attending the Dhyana. And as this flash does not aid us to analyse the hydrochloric acid gas, so the Ananda prevents us by startling us from perceiving the true nature of the phenomenon. In higher mystical states, then, we find that the Yogi or Magician has learnt how to suppress it.

"But the combination of the elements will usually be a definite single act of a catastrophic energy...The new consciousness resulting from the combination is, too, always a simple one."

VI

What is so important about these psychedelic drugs that we should give attention to them? Or devote time to what Crowley had to say years ago about them? Perhaps the most convenient answer to this question is to be found in a few statements made by some of the contemporaries named above.

In an essay entitled "Culture and the Individual" Aldous Huxley wrote emphatically:

"Unprecedentedly rapid technological and demographic changes are steadily increasing the dangers by which we are surrounded, and at the same time are steadily diminishing the relevance of the traditional feeling-and-behavior patterns imposed upon all individuals, rulers and ruled alike, by their culture. Always desirable, widespread training in the art of cutting holes in cultural fences is now the most urgent of necessities. Can such a training be speeded up and made more effective by a judicious use of the physically harmless psychedelics now available? On the basis of personal experience and the published evidence, I believe it can. In my utopian fantasy, *Island*, I speculated in fictional terms about the ways in which a substance akin to psilocybin could be used to potentiate the nonverbal education of adolescents and to remind adults that the real world is very different from the misshapen universe they have created for themselves by means of their culture-conditioned prejudices." And at this point, Huxley replied to some of his critical reviewers with rather deadly humor: "'Having Fun with Fungi'–that was how one waggish reviewer dismissed the matter. But which is better; to have Fun with Fungi or to have Idiocy with Idealogy, to have Wars because of Words, to have Tomorrow's Misdeeds out of Yesterday's Misdeeds?"

Then there is the significant passage in Alan Watts' book *The Joyous Cosmology*"

"The reaction of most cultured people to the idea of gaining any deep psychological or philosophical insight through a drug is that it is much too simple, too artificial, and even too banal to be seriously considered. A wisdom which can be "turned on" like the switch of a lamp seems to insult human dignity and degrade us to chemical automatons. One calls to mind pictures of a brave new world in which there is a class of synthesized Buddhas, of people who have been 'fixed' like the lobotomized, the sterilized, or the hypnotized, only in another direction..."

Whether the diehards and arch-conservatives of religious mysticism will like it or not, he proceeds to say:

"Despite the widespread and undiscriminating prejudice against drugs as such, and despite the claims of certain religious disciplines to be the sole means of genuine mystical insight, I can find no essential difference between the experiences induced, under favorable conditions, by these chemicals and the states of 'cosmic consciousness' recorded by R. M. Bucke, William James, Evelyn Underhill, Raynor Johnson and other investigators of mysticism...."

And finally, there is the clear, precise, and unequivocal testimony of Dr. Timothy Leary in his address "LSD–The Consciousness Expanding Drug":

"The non-game visionary experiences are, I submit, the key to behavior change–drug induced *satori*. In three hours under the right circumstances the cortex can be cleared. The games that frustrate and torment can be seen in the cosmic dimension. But the West has no ritual, no game to handle the CE (consciousness-expansion) drug experience. In the absence of relevant rituals we can only impose our familiar games, the politics of the nervous system, the mind controlling the brain...

"There are many methods for expanding consciousness beyond the game limit–Physical traumas can do it. Electrical shock. Extreme fatigue. Live in another and very different culture for a year where your roles and rituals and language just don't mean a thing. Or separate yourself from the game pressure by institutional withdrawal. Live for a while in a monastic cell. Or marry a Russian. Sensory deprivation does it...The most efficient way to cut through the game structure of Western life is the use of drugs, consciousness-expanding drugs..."

In order to arrive at any appreciation of the intrinsic worth of Crowley's essay *The Herb Dangerous*, the reader preferably should have had some type of "peak" or psychedelic experience himself. Only in this way, could he arrive at a sympathetic understanding of what Crowley, as well as our contemporaries, are trying to tell us. Failing that, then at the very least, he should be familiar with a few of what we can already call the classics of this new and ever-expanding literature.

For example, I would strongly recommend the following:
Religions, Values, and Peak Experiences – A. H. Maslow
Varieties of Religious Experience – Aldous Huxley
Doors of Perception – Aldous Huxley
Drugs and Mind – Dr. Robert S. de Ropp
LSD – The Consciousness-Expanding Drug – edited by David Solomon
The Joyous Cosmology – Alan Watts
My Self and I – Constance A. Newland
The Beyond Within – Sidney Cohen, M.D.

The entire topic of drug experimentation for psychedelic ends is dealt with in these books from various points of view. Some writers are wholly in favor of the wide employment of the new chemicals which include not merely lysergic acid, but mescaline, psilocybin and several other more recently synthesized ones. Most of the authors take a firm stand against any usage of the drugs outside of medically controlled institutions and research centers. A few others are more cautious–steering a mid-course between Scylla and Charybdis. A bird's eye view of the whole field and of current attitudes towards the consciousness-expanding drugs can, however, be thus obtained.

Dr. Sidney Cohen, in the book mentioned above, is very rational, avoiding the total condemnation of lysergic acid as do many of his medical colleagues, as well as the over-enthusiastic acceptance of it *a la Leary et al.*

He attempts to differentiate the "*drug-induced satori*" from both sanity and insanity by coining a new word "*unsanity*," which will do for the time being. His thorough-going rational attitude is expressed in this passage from his book:

> "Some of us quite understandably seeks out of the spiritual value of Rousseau's return to nature–with drugs if necessary. The answers are simple and at hand. All one needs is the faith to believe the mystic.
>
> "Few are willing to accept the alternative. The alternative is the recognition that we are an evolving species and that Final Truths are not discernible at this phase of our development. We must be satisfied with a willingness either to accept truths as sufficient to the day, or (and this is more difficult) to contemplate the questions without accepting answers."

I am quite certain that Crowley would have agreed with this sceptical viewpoint. But he would have added, on the basis of his own practical work with the mystical disciplines that "There is only one rock which Scepticism cannot shake; the Rock of Experience." And it was upon this rock that he built his edifice.

In addition to the above list, there is one book I should like to wholeheartedly recommend–*The Psychedelic Experience* by Timothy Leary and Richard Alpert, *et al.* I mention it apart from the others because it is the only single text which approximates, albeit distantly, the hashish essays of Crowley. The *Psychedelic Experience* is a do-it-yourself manual, predicated on the use of *The Tibetan Book of the Dead* edited by Dr. W. Y. Evans Wentz, as a psychopompic guide to the transcendental experience.

The authors deserve enormous commendation and great credit for the degree of insight and understanding evinced in this truly magnificent text–something quite novel and unique to our culture. Were Crowley alive today and familiar with this work, I am altogether confident that he would have immediately written a "rave" review of it in one of his *Equinox* publications. At the same moment of giving praise, he might also have directed attention to his own personal drug investigation, to the degree of excellence of his manifold instructions in the arts of meditation, magic, and tantra, and to an early attempt on his part at analysis of the specific effects of hashish. And for this, some would have called him egotistical.

Once having read some of the above-named books, I recommend turning to the second of the four essays of *The Herb Dangerous* by Oliver Haddo, published here, remembering that it was written fifty years ago. However, much of it is timeless. It may help to give form and direction to contemporary efforts to measure the extent and depth and action of the current psychedelic agents.

If I have repeated the claim that Crowley had the edge over most of our present-day researchers, it is primarily because we must do something to restore the historical balance, and to provide this generation with clear signposts and markers.

"Scientific Illuminism" was the phrase stamped on the front cover of every issue of *The Equinox* from 1909 to 1914. Accompanying this phrase were two others: "The Aim of Religion. The Method of Science." At various times, Crowley was called upon to elaborate what he meant by these phrases. Perhaps the best exposition is to be found in an Editorial he wrote for one of the issues of *The Equinox*:

"1. We perceive in the sensible world, Sorrow. Ultimately that is: we admit the Existence of a problem requiring Solution.

"2. We accept the proofs of Hume, Kant, Herbert Spencer, Fuller, and other of this thesis:

"The Ratiocinative Faculty or Reason of Man contains in its essential nature an element of self-contradition.

"3. Following on this, we say:

"If any resolution there be of these two problems, the Vanity of Life and the Vanity of Thought, it must be in attainment of a Consciousness which transcends both of them. Let us call this super-normal consciousness, or for want of a better name, 'Spiritual Experience.'

"4. Faith has been proposed as a remedy. But we perceive many incompatible forms of Faith founded on Authority–The Vedas, The Auran, The Bible, Buddha, Christ, Joseph Smith. To chose between them we must resort to reason, already shown to be a fallacious guide.

"5. There is only one rock which Scepticism cannot shake; the Rock of Experience.

"6. We have therefore endeavored to eliminate from the conditions of acquiring Spiritual Experience its dogmatic, theological, accidental, climatic and other inessential elements.

"7. We require the employment of a strictly scientific method. The mind of the seeker must be unbiased; all prejudice and other sources of error must be perceived as such and extirpated.

"8. We have therefore devised a Syncretistic-Eclectic Method combining the essentials of all methods, rejecting all their trammels, to attack the Problem, through exact experiments and not by guesses.

"9. For each pupil we recommend a different method (in detail) suited to his needs; just as a physician prescribes the medicine proper to each particular patient.

"10. We further believe that the Consummation of Spiritual Experience is reflected into the spheres of intellect and action as Genius, so that by taking an ordinary man we can by training produce a Master.

"This Thesis requires proof; we hope to supply such proof by producing Genius to order."

Corroboration is still necessary: but it is not entirely outside the bounds of possibility. It seems to me that the day is at hand when Crowley and what he stood for should obtain some tardy recognition. For entirely too long a period of time has this man been maligned and villified on the most stupid or invalid grounds–grounds today which would hardly be justified by the ordinary intelligent person. This has resulted in the by-passing of his considerable accomplishments in the realm of mysticism. It has resulted in our ignoring his rude exposure of the psycho-social booby-traps into which we have aimlessly wandered, as though he had never put them on record. We are the losers thereby.

What were his qualifications? Some of these have already been delineated. In addition, he had received a fine classical and scientific education at Cambridge. Further, in his mountaineering exploits in Scotland, the Swiss Alps and the Himalayas, he had demonstrated a peculiar kind of what some considered to be a foolhardy courage accompanied by a special type of caution, both of which characteristics were especially useful when he came to tackle the problem of the psychedelic drugs. This was also depicted in his usually solitary walks across Spain in 1908 when this sort of thing was hardly popular, and across boundaries of the Sahara Desert and Algeria in 1909 as well as many times later, climbing several of the extinct volcanoes in Mexico, and hiking across the lower borders of China adjoining Vietnam with a wife and child. All this was done during a period of early twentieth century history which was not in the least bit as safe-transportation wise–as it is today. Topping these accomplishments, he was a superb prose writer as these and other essays indicate, and a fine lyrical poet.

Furthermore, and this is far and away the most important consideration here, Crowley was an experimental mystic of the highest magnitude. He had practiced yoga and magical techniques assiduously for many years until he has achieved a thorough-going master over both Eastern and Western methods. All of these rare skills were eventually brought to bear on his experimentation with a variety of drugs. These essays bear witness to, and provide massive evidence of, his objectives and scientific attitude to the whole process. For instance:

"One single trained observer with five years' work, less money than would build a bakehouse, and no more help than his dozen of volunteer students could give him, would earn him self a fame loftier than the stars, and set mankind on the royal road to the solution of the One great problem. Scientific Illuminism would have deserved its name, or mysticism would have received a blow which would save another young fool like myself from wasting his whole life on so senseless a study and enable him to engage in the nobler career of cheating and duping his fellows in the accredited spheres of commerce and politics, to say nothing of the grosser knaveries of the liberal professions.

"But I have no doubts. Let the investigator study his own brain on the lines I have laid down, possibly in the first place with the aid of hashish or some better physical expedient to overcome the dull scepticism which is begotten of idleness upon ignorance; it is useless to study the no-brain of another, on the strength of a reputation for fraud, as the spiritualism investigators seem to do. Your own brain is the best; next, the trained and vigorous brains of clever and educated men, in perfect health, honest and wary."

This, I think, will demonstrate clearly and adequately some of the motives Crowley had in writing about his experiences with hashish.

VII

An enormous bibliography relative to lysergic acid is in process of creation. Various of the authors contributing to the Solomon's book, for example, list as many as seventy odd titles. These include books, papers, essays, articles, etc. However, McGlothlin* in his essays on the subject, declares that since the discovery of its manifold psychic effects in the year 1943, more than 700 papers have been published on lysergic acid.

This unusually wide interest was at first stimulated by hopes within the psychiatric field of producing a model schizophrenia which could be helpful in the study of the commonly occurring mental illnesses. This anticipation was subsequently abandoned when it was found that there were enormous differences between the two psychic states. In place, however, of the hope of a model psychosis, there have developed techniques of employing the drug as an aid to the psychotherapy of the more intractable psychoneuroses. There is evidence that success is being achieved in this direction. Constance Newland's book

---

* *Long-lasting Effects of LSD on Certain Attitudes in Normals: An Experimental Proposal.* William H. McGlothlin, The Rand Corporation, Santa Monica, California, 1962.

My Self and I is on particular indication of what has been attempted here.

In my own case, the psychedelics were responsible not only for several shaking peak-experiences, but even more important, as the "thrill" of unfamiliarity wore off, some profound insights that had altogether eluded me despite many years of intensive depth therapy. If for no other reason than this, there is great value in these chemical agents. Nor am I alone in this realization. Several psychologists of the various analytical schools have had similar revealing experiences, though because of the current legal situation, some are not willing to expose themselves to punitive social action by declaring this fact and placing their own experience on record.

Rather more conclusive than this, however, has been the discovery that alcoholism is by far the most common pathology to respond favorably to the drug. The Canadian psychiatrists were, I believe, among the first to perceive this fact and to experiment with the drug with satisfactory results. Several reports have been written, sparked by Humphrey Osmond, D.P.M.

But what has actually triggered the vast public interest in lysergic acid was the discovery that (a) intense pleasurable feelings were stimulated and released during the drug experience, and that (b) transcendental mystical states were stimulated.

The first reaction has led to the beatnik involvement on the University campus and elsewhere, with massive bootlegging of the drug for use, unfortunately by pubescents and early adolescents. These people have no earthly justification for such experimentation–not at least until they have established themselves in some kind of solid involvement in the socio-economic order in which they find themselves. Otherwise, it is neurotic escape, pure and simple, as well as the expression of their revolt against family and society.

Youngsters have the right to rebel against the established order of things. Theirs is not only the right to rebel, but rebellion is inherent in their very structure. To the adolescent, society is hopefully bogged down in a worn-out set of useless attitudes, activities, and institutions. None of them seems to appeal overmuch to the adolescent of today.

Given the passage of two decades, and imperceptibly these people will have become part of the social order against which previously they have rebelled. It has changed because of their earlier non-conformity, yet curiously it remains the same. And then it may seem to them that despite all the criticisms legitimately to be made, there are phases of society that persist because of their survival value. This being so, we should permit and even encourage the younger person in his growth and rebellion, but we must nonetheless guard him against possible damage to his own personal usefulness later on.

I suggest the rebel would do better in his rebellion against society by burrowing from within. Acquire all the "tools" society has to offer, and then, in the process of adaptation, employ these tools to modify or destroy what is meaningless or useless in society. But to use the psychedelics as a means of rebelling, of undercutting society, is hardly the most intelligent use of the psychedelic drugs. To "drop out" of the struggle for existence is idiocy of the most grotesque kind.

The use of lysergic acid, or any other hallucinogenic agent, merely for "kicks", as has been suggested as the freest, most spontaneous attitude for experimentation, sounds far too much like the irresponsible attitude of some present-day high school kids. One's first and immediate reaction is purely negative. It would seem to constitute an abuse of the drug.

Yet, alcohol is used for this purpose today. For the most part, it is a socially acceptable drug, and despite some national concern about alcoholism, not too very much is made of this disease, for so it has come to be currently considered–or when the ordinary sober person goes off on an occasional "bender'" at a party.

Conventional society provides many avenues to the average man or woman for "kicks." Driving a car is commonly used for this purpose quite apart from the prosaic notion of transportation. The price in deaths on the highway runs to staggeringly high figures.

Business activity may be used not merely to provide for the exchange of goods and services, but it is often used as a means of getting a "kick" out of life. It is not altogether condemned for that purpose–even though the price frequently paid is coronary disease and the gastric ulcer.

Many responsible physicians have called frequent attention to some of the adverse sequellae of the psychedelic drugs. Suicides, depressed and anxious reactions, psychotic breakdowns and neurotic exacerbations are amongst these side effects. The toll amongst neurotic adolescents is undeniably heavy. The use of lysergic acid is not altogether without serious dangers, and some unwise people are bound to suffer irrevocably. To deny this is to put blinkers in front of one's eyes and demonstrate a high degree of personal and social irresponsibility.

There is a price to be paid for the use of drugs–though this need not be necessarily a major and over-riding objection. It is simply a factor to be recognized.

It should certainly not be toyed with by him who runs and reads. It needs to be administered by experts trained in the use of drugs–preferably by a sympathetic psychiatrist and attended by a psychologist or some other person really experienced in the role and duties of a "psycho-pomp." Admittedly, there are some lay people who have acquired extensive experience in the art of "psychedelic baby-sitting." But things being what they are, and the legal and medical situations as it is, the experimenter needs to be watched during and after the "trip" by competent and professional people.

It is no use denying, as some foolishly have done, that there have been mishaps following upon the ingestion of lysergic acid. Aspirin, for example, sometimes causes fatality, and so has penicillin–and many other useful drugs. The better part of wisdom and valor would dictate that due acknowledgement be made of this fact, and be guided accordingly. But the fact that accidents do occur and will surely continue to occur, is of itself not sufficient an argument to warrant the discontinuance of lysergic acid. It is going to be used legitimately or otherwise, legally or illicitly. But those who are ill-advised to use it illicitly, and without proper guidance, have only themselves to blame if they come to harm.

"The grounds for any possible suppression of these medicines are almost entirely superstitious." So wrote Alan Watts. "There is no evidence for their being as deleterious as alcohol or tobacco, nor indeed, for their being harmful in any way except when used in improper circumstances, or, perhaps, with psychotic subjects. They are considerably less dangerous than many of the ordinary contents of the family medicine cupboard or kitchen closet...Speaking quite strictly, mystical insight is no more in the chemical than biological knowledge is in the microscope."

It is worth while taking note of a set of observations made by Crowley in the twenties, when much of his most mature writing was done:

> "Intoxication, that is, ecstasy, is the Key to Reality...Religious ecstasy is necessary to man's soul. Where this is attained by mystical practices, directly, as it should be, people need no

substitutes. Thus the Hindus remain contentedly sober, and care nothing for the series of invaders who have occupied their country from time to time and governed them. But where the only means of obtaining this ecstasy, or a simulacrum of it, known to the people in alcohol, they must have alcohol. Deprive them of wine, or beer, or whatever their natural drink may be, and they replace it by morphia, cocaine, or something easier to conceal, and to take without detection.

"Stop that, and it is Revolution. As long as man can get rid of his surplus Energy in enjoyment, he finds life easy and submits. Deprive him of Pleasure, or Ecstasy, and his mind begins to worry about the way in which he is exploited and oppressed. Very soon he begins furtively to throw bombs; and, gathering strength, to send his tyrants to the gallows."

So appropriate do these warnings appear, that my mind harks back automatically to the grim era of the Volstead Act. During the 1920s in the United States, millions of otherwise decent and law-abiding citizens went out of their way to show their utter contempt for the Prohibition legislation. Even those who, previously, had used little or no alcoholic beverages found themselves drawn willy-nilly into this maelstrom of law-defiance. The Federal agencies set up to enforce the observance of the law discovered an obstinate confrontation by a wilful and determined citizenry aided and abetted unfortunately by gangster elements which had found the brewing, distillation and distribution of intoxicating drinks far more lucrative than a gold mine.

Eventually, the Act had to be repealed. But it was only after heaven alone knows how many peoples' health had suffered from drinking bootlegged whiskey and other drinks, and vast wealth had been squandered fruitlessly in both breaking and enforcing an unpopular law. Furthermore, it inaugurated a period when respect for the law fell to an all-time low, and I do not think we have yet fully recovered. This is the anarchy Crowley seems to refer to above.

Something similar is about to occur on a contemporary basis. Regardless of a few unverified scientific findings about the danger to body and mind involved in the use the psychedelic drugs, too vast an impact has been made on all levels of society for an easy halt to be engineered. If laws must be passed, then they should be oriented primarily for the protection of the minor–certainly not to deprive the so-called adult population of satisfactory emotional outlets through means which possess but little danger. If this is not respected, the lawlessness of the 20s may be experienced by a new generation.

Random reports indicate that over one million adults have to-date experienced the psychedelic drugs, including scores or more of medical doctors and psychotherapists. Many priests and ministers have affirmed the experience as profoundly religious or transcendental. For them, faith has been replaced by personal experience.

This other reaction (b) has engaged the attention of some of the finest speculative minds that our generation has seen–from Aldous Huxley and Alan Watts to Richard Alpert and Timothy Leary.

Since the latter two psychologists were expelled in controversy from Harvard–intense public interest has revolved about all their activities. The have written and lectured widely on the subject, whipping the already deep interest in lysergic acid into a national preoccupation. So vast has the latter become that several states have legislated against the possession of the hallucinogenic drugs, though the Federal government cautiously has held hearings concerning the advisability of so doing. The last word has not yet been said, of this I am quite certain. We are too close to what is happening. But if I may be permitted to hazard a guess, I would suggest that the above writers may yet go down in psycho-religious history as outstanding figures who have been instrumental in transforming current, dead religious attitudes into vital mystical experience. This could result, on the other hand, in increased membership in the several religious institutions in the country–for which I am quite certain the churches will never express appreciation–and in a revived experimental attitude towards the whole topic of mysticism which has never been equalled before in the known history of mankind. In any event, the latter will leaven the public religions, and transform them. The result of all hits may prove to be the final vindication of Aleister Crowley, and of what he came to call his system of "Scientific Illuminism."

A half century has elapsed since he coined this phrase. Today, only a few people are in the least bit aware of the superb analytical writing produced by Crowley. With lysergic acid practically a byword on so many lips, and when so much excellent writing pro and con has appeared, it seems to me imperative to revive the original study by Crowley. He had so much to say in this connection and he has said it very well. Moreover, because of his training, experience, and mystical accomplishments, he was in a far better position to articulate what he did than most of our contemporaries. This is hardly to decry our present-day writers. They have done, on the positive side of the ledger, a yeoman job to indicate that the prudent use of psychedelic drugs may vastly expand the limited horizon of the human mind.

VIII

One of the several sticks with which Crowley was attacked by his contemporaries was the sexual one. Crowley had developed his own ideas about sex and sexual more which he was not in the least bashful or reticent in talking about. He wrote them prolifically for anybody who could read. They were to the effect that the social and moral inhibitions and restrictions of his day were a crime against nature for which a severe toll would be enacted. Not wholly unlike Playboy's philosophy of sex, for which Heffner has been widely extolled and abused, they were far ahead of his time.

Crowley was a bit scattered. That is to say, much of the thinking, precise and beautifully expressed though it may have been, is diffused throughout many volumes. He was never really able to elaborate his lifetime philosophy in a single clear volume. Though he did attempt this, it was in symbolic and poetic language, occasionally in archaic literary styles, so that it missed its purpose of common elucidation for the public almost wholly.

For example, he meant *Liber Aleph* or *The Book of Wisdom or Folly*, written possibly in 1917-18 and published posthumously by his disciples, to be a mature statement of his final philosophy and attitude towards those matters, including sex, which had preoccupied him all his life. But the book was couched in an archaic form which undoubtedly required enormous skill and concentration to write on his part. Reading it for most people is not calculated to win him ardent disciples nor to favorably influence his enemies. Following after the short paragraph opening this Introduction, there is another, continuing the same theme:

> "But I make Effort in vain, O my Son, to record this Matter in Detail: for it is the Quality of this Grass to Quicken the Operation of Thought it may be a Thousandfold, and moreover to figures each Step in Images complex and overpowering in Beauty, so that one hath not Time wherein to conceive, much less to utter, any Word for a Name of any one of them."

I have stated that his liberal attitudes relative to sex are not unlike those of Heffner as published in *Playboy*. But this is not all. He meaningfully related sex to mysticism, arguing that the ecstasy of one was not too dissimilar to the ecstasy of the other, and that one could be casually connected to the other. He once wrote, simply and sincerely:

"When you have proved that God is merely a name for the sex instinct, it appears to me not far to the perception that the sex instinct is God."

On the basis of his wide world travel, with its undoubted vast opportunity for sexual experience and experiment, he wrote some technical instructions on rendering this relationship effective. They became part and parcel of the particular mystico-magical philosophy that he came to elaborate–piecemeal, for it took many years for his experience to fill in many theoretical gaps in what he was originally taught. This may be one of the several reasons why so many of them are couched in symbolic form, a form from which many people have retreated–defeated. But there is really little need for retreat or defeat. A little meditation, a little illumination (with or without psychedelics) and the door swings wide open to reveal an ineffable brilliance.

I was therefore excited when I read in the September, 1966 issue of *Playboy* an interview with Timothy Leary. It almost seemed to me a flashback to fifty years ago–with Crowley being interviewed, but this time in a sympathetic environment, not by a group of stupid, hostile reporters who wrote for John Bull and the sensation-mongering group of newspapers owned by Lord Beaverbrook.

For example, Leary has stated in that interview: "The sexual impact is, of course, the open but private secret about LSD, which none of us has talked about in the last few years. It's socially dangerous enough to say that LSD helps you find divinity and helps you discover yourself. You're already in trouble when you say that. But then if you announce that the psychedelic experience is basically, a *sexual* experience, you're asking to bring the whole middle-aged, middle-class monolith down on your head...The sexual ecstasy is the basic reason for the current LSD boom. When Dr. Goddard, the head of the Food and Drug Administration, announced in a Senate hearing that ten percent of our college students are taking LSD, did you ever wonder why? Sure, they're discovering God and meaning; sure, they're discovering themselves; but did you really think that sex wasn't the fundamental reason for this surging youthful social boom? You can no more do research on LSD and leave out sexual ecstasy than you can do microscopic research on tissue and leave out cells...The LSD session, you see, is an overwhelming awakening of experience; it releases potent, primal energies, and one of these is the sexual impulse, which is the strongest impulse at any level of organic life..."

Even a hasty perusal of Crowley's literary output will reveal similar notions, preoccupations and conclusions. But he carried them far beyond this simple theme to the experience of the identity of God and sexual ecstasy.

IX

At the time when Crowley wrote about these topics, the legal situation was far different from now. At that time, many of the then-known hallucinogenic drugs could be purchased without much difficulty in the open market–from the nearest pharmacy. Earlier, de Quincy had described this open situation at some length in his *Confessions of An English Opium Eater*. Nowadays, all of this has changed. Some of these drugs are not even available to a licensed physician. Only an occasional clinic or institute devoted to research is able to obtain, for example, lysergic acid.

That there is an extensive black market in lysergic acid and marihuana is well-known. I have learned in Northern California there is such an open black market that is possible to place an order for lysergic acid and get a dozen capsules–each of three hundred micrograms–within a half an hour. However, there are stringent laws against possession and disposing of these psychedelic drugs. *Caveat emptor!*

Sooner or later the question is going to be raised "Where then do we get these psychedelic drugs? I am quite sure that someone is going to write me a letter, assuming that I possess some and am willing to distribute some, and so ask for several doses.

At the outset, therefore, *let me state unequivocally that I have none of these psychedelic drugs and have no access to them.* My personal experience with lysergic acid date back some years and when I participated gratefully, in a research project with a local psychiatrist. At that time I took four "trips" which I count among the most valuable and memorable experiences of a lifetime. *But I am not now a source for the psychedelics nor have I ever been.*

What then, can I recommend the reader, knowing that most of these research projects have been cut back? Black market? Hardly. That is certainly not the best solution to the problem of need. When Leary was asked this question in the Playboy interview, he answered rather cautiously: "LSD is against the law, and I certainly would not advise anyone to violate the law. I will say this, however: Throughout human history, men who have wanted to expand their consciousness, to find deeper meaning inside themselves, have been able to do it if they were willing to commit the time and energy to do so. In other times and countries, men would walk barefooted 2000 miles to find spiritual teachers who would turn them on to Buddha, Mohammed or Ramakrishna."

Apart from the legal considerations, there is the ever-present doubt of the essential purity of the black-market product. More likely than not, it is bound to have been adulterated for possible financial gain, now that the criminal syndicates have seen an opening for vast profits. And what effect on health and other factors the possible adulterations may have can be left to anyone's imagination.

About the only thing that can be safely recommended today is wide inquiry relative to research enterprises. The Veterans Administration in its various facilities all over the country is forever experimenting and conducting research and investigation of the value of this and many another drug. It could be contacted with a view to ascertaining if volunteers are needed. The agency of the Armed Services that always conducts experiments in chemical agents for war purposes and for defense against attack may also require volunteers. It is possible, however, that such volunteers are mainly recruited from duly enlisted members of the various branches of the Armed Services. Mental hospitals in the various states of this country likewise may be engaged in research programs where this and similar psychedelic drugs are investigated. The hospitals connected with many Universities are committed to research for which volunteers are always needed. It seems to me, therefore, that in such medical facilities as those just described, lie the best possibilities for gaining legal access to experimentation with the psychedelic drugs.

Moreover, personal experimentation should be under expert supervision–and this I think is most important. Investigating the reaction of these psychedelic drugs without competent assistance is in my estimation stupidity of the most grotesque kind. On the other hand, evidence supports the idea that medical supervision is not necessarily the most advantageous kind of guidance. Perhaps in due course of time, the authorities who handle this research may come to realize, with Leary and Crowley and many others, that the best guide in this sense is the person who has been "there" several times himself. It may well be that as the more sensational type of publicity dies down, and a more serious attitude sets in, this counsel may come to be recognized. It may also transpire that other facilities will eventuate which may make it more possible for mature, intelligent, and progressive persons to partake of the benefits and advantages of the psychedelic experience.

In this connection, I must register part of an interview with a relatively unknown Los Angeles poet, Charles Bukowski, in the Los Angeles Free Press, March 3, 1967, when he was asked his opinion about lysergic acid.

"I think that everything should be made available to everybody, and I mean LSD, cocaine, grass, opium, the works. Nothing on earth available to man should be confiscated and made unlawful by other men in more seemingly powerful and advantageous positions...I grow tired of the 18th century moralities in a 20th century space-atomic age. If I want to kill myself I feel that should be my business; if I want to get hooked on the mainline that should be my business. If I go out and hold up gas stations at night to pay for my supply it is because the law inflates a very cheap thing into an escalated war against my nerves and my soul. The law is wrong; I am right.

"What more can you do with the dead than kill them? Look at our safe, undrugged populace now in the busses, at the sporting-events, in the supermarkets, and tell me if they are a pleasant sight. And why should the M.D.s be the dolers out of goodies? Aren't they fat enough now? Wealthy enough? Spoiled enough?...

"My objection to the current LSD-craze-phase-blaze, the dull-heads as a kind of primitive stomping ground, as a substitute for the soul...Being unable to take the truth, being unable to face an honest mirror, they PLAY AT SOUL, at being IN, bob, boot, beard, beret, hip, opo, anything. Long hair, short skirts, sandals, anything, psychedelic parties, paintings, music, psychedelic grapefruit, psychedelic guerrilla frong, opo cups, shades, bikes, yogi, psychic lightsounds, disco, girls are Richards, fuzz now Soap, Kid Goldstein the super pop new boy, The Jefferson Airplane, Hell's Angels, anything, any damn thing to give them identity, to give them a facade of Being to Cover the Horrible Hole. Bob Dylan is their soul: 'Something's happening and you don't know what it is, do you Mr. Jones?"...

"Or a group of them down on the floor in a circle and pass the grass and talk about Leary and the good old Left, talk about Andy Warhol, and how horrible the war in Vietnam is, and only a damn fool can hold a job, and who wants to drive? —walking is better. And somebody ought to shoot Johnson. And there are candles on the floor. And the boys are mother's boys, and the women are twice-married, twice-divorces, grey, bitter and in their mid-forties. Don't think! Freak-in. Freak-out. Lights, LSD. Leary, Guitars, Love...

"Not all their ideas are totally without merit but in the essence of all thinking alike on like subjects they cover the Horrible Hole, they imagine themselves objective, lovable human beings...But really they are one big shit-mind of jelly grabbing at LSD like the Holy Cross and making me hate it because of their footprints, their mindprints are across my eyesight. Maybe when they move on to their next hype I will test a little acid. Until then, let them wallow in it until they get a pigbellyfull."

This is almost like hearing the ghost of Crowley of forty years ago laughing ribaldly down the dark corridors of time.

X

In the meantime, until some reliable and legitimate sources for the psychedelics are discovered, there is much that the proposed experimenter can do. No drug alone or psychospiritual technique can eradicate the basic insecurity that lurks in the depths of the human psyche. This fact has to be faced some time, and actually should be faced prior to any hallucinogenic excursion. It is for this and similar reasons that I have long insisted that the student of the Mysteries should precede his practical experiments with a more or less lengthy familiarity on the couch with one of the other forms of psychotherapy. Whether it is Freudian, Jungian, Reichian or any other variation of the basic psychoanalytic school makes little difference. The analytical experience will at least have brought the student in touch with aspects and functions and contents of his own psyche that he might otherwise have never known. Whether the neurotic problem is resolved by this process really becomes a secondary consideration. It is the honest attempt to come face to face with oneself which is paramount. Beyond all other things, it will also result in the exposure of any latent psychosis, and separate the frankly neurotic from outright psychotic person. The latter then should be sternly counselled to never, under any circumstances, touch the psychedelic drugs.

What I would be particularly interested in is a tentative marriage of the Reichian non-verbal system of vegeto-therapy with the occasional and judicious use of lysergic acid. The former system is dedicated to the dissolution of the neuro-muscular character armor-a technical term indicating all the ego's defenses on both the psychic and muscular levels of function. Since one of the effects of lysergic acid is apparently to dissolve the fixed boundaries of the ego, it seems to me that the joint use of both would be synergistic. Each would facilitate the efficacy of the other, pointing the way to the peak-experience. in this way, time and effort and money–all vital factors in psychotherapy–would be saved, no mean feat.

Psychotherapy will also have exposed the student to his own concealed inferiorities, insecurities, fears and doubts as nothing else will. When this has been accomplished, whatever subsequently may emerge during the psychedelic experience will hardly be as terrifying and overwhelming as the records indicate it has been for some. According to Gerald Heard, the greater the ego–implying that purely unconscious fears and guilts have been compensated for by a hypertrophy, as it were, of the ego-function-the more severe will the period of terror elicited by lysergic acid. Before the sublime moments and the ecstatic experience of expansion can come and go, the ego must give up and, willingly or not, dissolve. This is the traditional surrender of the ego before the "mystical marriage" can occur.

For those who resist ego-dissolving, this process, the temporary "dying" induced by the three little pillules of 150 micrograms of lysergic acid, can be a devilish experience. It is no wonder that the bibliographies refer to a certain small percentage going through psychotic episodes as a result of a trip with lysergic acid. Fortunately, in my case, I had had years of psychotherapy prior to the first experience with the hallucinogens, so that I was spared this horror. But–according to Alan Harrington, who wrote "*A Visit to Inner Space*," one of the essays collected by David Solomon in his book *LSD–the Consciousness Expanding Drug*, already referred to–he was so concerned with hanging on to himself that he missed initially a great deal of the beauty. Though he hastens to add that once the surrender was consummated, he ascended to "the top of the universe" like everybody else.

I shall never forget an occasion of several years ago when I "baby-sat" for a colleague about to take his first "trip," as part of the psychiatric research project in which we had both participated. About an hour after ingesting the three tiny pills, he began to experience a mild chill, gentle at first, but growing in intensity until his teeth chattered furiously. From then on, until the end of the trip many hours later, he was afflicted by a host of severe gastro-intestinal symptoms, retching, vomiting and diarrhoea. The trip merely intensified his current neurotic symptoms. They were present before the trip, and no doubt are still active. He was truly a piteous sight. The drug had stripped him practically of all his protective armor–and his righteousness was as rags. From that day forward, he was intellectually opposed even to the possibility of lysergic acid being considered an adjunct or a catalytic agent in psychotherapy or research of any kind. He had had it!

It was not until long afterwards, during a reflection upon the psychedelic agents together with the remark of Gerald Heard, and, meditation upon my own and other people's experiences, that I realized how valid the Heard judgement is. The colleague was really attempting to hang on to himself by the "skin of his teeth." In spite of all other appearances, he was terrified to let go of himself. For this role-playing, he paid a very high price–the extent of which even he had not and could not recognize at the time.

Mention must also be made at this time of the commonly asserted thesis that Mysticism is an escape and a substitute for sexually frustrated energies. One often hears people, without direct knowledge of either Mysticism or the psychedelic experience, refer to both of them as escapes. These are glib phrases, often used by writers in the popular press. Of course, this attitude expresses the conservative theme, usually being uttered either to maintain the status quo or to conceal their own fear and inner bankruptcy.

On the one hand, the indiscriminate use of the hallucinogens by adolescents certainly argues their irresponsible substitution for life and living experience. A fantasy life, no matter how triggered, is a feeble substitute for reality, and no matter how ineffable the ecstasy, or vivid the imagery, or keen the senses during a "trip," the ability to handle life, people and the world is bound inevitably to suffer. One pays a very high price, adaptation-wise for "escape."

David Solomon, the editor of the collection of essays on lysergic acid previously referred to, in describing his own "trip" avers that the drug did induce a flight, but in this case a flight directly into reality. This was no escape in any literal or conventional sense of the word. He states that he had never before seen, or sensed in any way, a personal unity and involvement with the concrete material world which, under the impact of this sensory expansion, took on another meaning. His experience brought him to perceive that there is not a material world with enormous tones and overtones of which we are but rarely aware. His was no evasive flight from, but a deep probe, into reality. And–very much like Crowley fifty years before–he comments that his drug-accelerated mind did not merely grasp the symbolic poetic import, the utter simplicity and truth of Blake's ecstatic vision. For the first time in his life he literally saw "the world in a grain of sand."

In conclusion, the final question asked by the interviewer of Leary in *Playboy* should be repeated: "How will this psychedelic regimen enrich human life?" Leary's answer, simple and eloquent, is one that Crowley also might have respected and approved of.

> "It will enable each person to realize that he is not a gameplaying robot put on this planet to be given a Social Security number and to be spun on the assembly line of school, career,

insurance, funeral, goodbye. Through LSD, each human being will be taught to understand that the entire history of evolution is recorded inside his body; the challenge of the complete human life will be for each person to recapitulate and experientially explore every aspect and vicissitude of this ancient and majestic wilderness. Each person will become his own Buddha, his own Einstein, his own Galileo. Instead of relying on canned, static, dead knowledge passed on from other symbol producers, he will be using his span of 80 or so years on this planet to live out every possibility of the human, prehuman and even subhuman adventure. As more respect and time are diverted to these explorations, he will be less hung upon trivial, external pastimes. And this may be the natural solution to the problem of leisure. When all the heavy work and mental drudgery are taken over by machines, what are we going to do with ourselves–build even bigger machines? The obvious and only answer to this peculiar dilemma is that we are going to have to explore the infinity of inner space, to discover the terror and adventure and ecstasy that lie within us all."

If man is to achieve inner peace, which could and must lead to world harmony, he must do so according to his own inner nature. This must be explored. Then he might become capable of achieving what he already is potentially. "Every man and every woman is a star."

The process of self-realization releases the unifying energy needed for harmonious relationships with the world at large and all things and people therein. Beneath all our contemporary violence and sensationalism, a wave of the future is already in evidence. A momentum is being generated in the direction of aiding man to fulfill his deepest potentials. The peak experience–whether spontaneous or induced through the various methods briefly discussed in this essay–produces a release of energy from the unconscious parts of the psyche leading to the realization of these inherent possibilities.

This was Crowley's lifelong thesis; thus his insistence that the mystic state be studied by scientific men without prejudice and without further delay.

MY ROSICRUCIAN ADVENTURE
New Falcon Publications, Third Revised Edition, 2017

*A personal account of the
Hermetic Order of the Golden Dawn*

Originally written in the mid-1930s to serve as an introduction to the four volumes of *The Golden Dawn* published by The Aries Press (Chicago, 1936-40), it soon became evident that this intended essay was entirely too large, too personal and too rambling to fulfill it's required purpose. At the suggestion of the late George Engelke, who then operated the Aries Press, it was published as a separate volume, to stand wholly by itself, and to serve as a companion volume to *The Golden Dawn*.

It had been my intention to employ a typical Order ritual phrase for the title–*Konx Om Pax*. Many decades ago, however, this phrase had already been employed by Aleister Crowley as a title to one of his several books. In the Order rituals, the words "Konx Om Pax" are preceded first by "Khabs Am Pekht", and succeeded by "Light in Extension"–all three phrases being equivalent in meaning but in three different languages. The second of the three did not strike me as being suitable for a title. This left the last phrase, which I decided to use.

In the advertising material at the end of the original edition of this book *My Rosicrucian Adventure*, p. 141 *et seq.*, the Introduction to *The Golden Dawn* was described as "practically a verbatim reprint of 'Light in Extension'." Several doubts still lingered regarding the suitability of this phrase. After further reflection I decided to reject outright the idea of using an Order ritual phrase, and to use a title more descriptive of my own personal experience with the Order. Thus, the final selection of the title–*My Rosicrucian Adventure*.

A modified version finally came to be employed as the Introduction to *The Golden Dawn*. A large part of the second and third chapters were omitted, the remaining ones slightly edited, with a few pieces of new material inserted on the subject of initiation and its meaning.

In the original edition there were some colossal and appalling misprints and typographical errors. Every author of course is subject to this nightmare, but so far as *My Rosicrucian Adventure* is concerned, I can only say that at the time of publication no galley proofs were ever furnished. The publisher simply proceeded with book production, and presented me with the *fait accompli*. Ordinarily, I would not have minded. To be spared the tedium of some of these literary chores is nothing short of a divine blessing, but many of these errors were so glaring and so serious as to pervert the meaning of the text. As for example, *Death* was printed for the Qabalistic word *Daath* about a half dozen times! This made no sense at all. Those students who had previously acquired some Qabalistic knowledge would be in no quandary at all relative to meaning. It was the newcomer to this material who would be presented with a really perplexing situation. I am enormously relieved that these errors have finally been taken care of.

One more matter finally needs to be considered. It should be abundantly clear upon reading this book and two others mentioned in the Postscript, that one of the several reasons for the debacle that ultimately overtook the Hermetic Order of the Golden Dawn was the ridiculous quest for Masters, Secret Chiefs of inner plane contacts. This is a pandemic blight that has devastated other more popular and populous movements before this. It is particularly tragic in the case of the Golden Dawn because the goals of the Great Work were so clearly delineated and a technique for its attainment so adequately provided. That was the attainment of the knowledge and conversation of the Holy Guardian Angel or the quest for the Higher and Divine Genius.

Nowhere in any of the initiatory oaths or rituals is the search for Masters mentioned. It is only an enlarged or inflated ego–which really conceals a dismal inferiority and insecurity–that demands such a quest. The disease in modern times was first seen developing in the Theosophical Society when several members who felt that they were being ignored or neglected by Madame Blavatsky and her Teachers instituted a search for the latter, first among mediums and clairvoyants, and then by other means. Though all of these ended in ignominy and in "revelations" of the most complete balderdash, the movement spread–and amongst other organizations reached the Golden Dawn. Here the results were truly devastating.

If there be Masters or Secret Chiefs here or elsewhere, then it seems self-evident they have to be recognized as having enough horse-sense or insight to perceive through the exercise of their own powers who is worthy of being introduced to their Community of Light. If they cannot perceive the light shining from the truly aspiring student whose goals are high, whose abilities are considerable, and who might prove to be useful to their eternal cause, then they are not worth bothering with. Certainly to hunt for such adepts whose insight is so defective is a pure waste of time and energy.

It is only an inflated ego which refuses to consider this conclusion and send one off hunting for those inner plane contacts, so-called. Francis King's *Ritual Magic in England* (the American edition is entitled *Secret Rites of Occult Magic*, MacMillan, N.Y. 1971) gives ample testimony to the sterility and stupidity of the several Order groups, dedicated to this end. He also notes correctly that communications from such sources are usually grossly inferior to those an ordinarily intelligent person might pen. For some time, around 1935, I attended meetings conducted by one of the most elderly adepts of an English Temple. The "North Men"–Masters from the North–were invoked, but what they eventually delivered was so inconsequential and drivel-like as to leave no permanent impress on my memory today.

The problem of ego-hypertrophy being that which is to be coped with, several considerations arise. Very rarely is it dealt with except in moralistic terms, which however are not the significant factors. Nor is the inner problem realistically handled by declining to employ the pronoun "I" in everyday speech.

It may or may not be common knowledge, but involved in the inflated or hypertrophied ego is a vast series of emotional factors allied with feelings of insecurity and inferiority, usually totally unconscious. That is to say that though conscious at one time, they have been pushed into the dark area of the unconscious psyche, out of sight. The enlarged ego is thus an attempt at compensation for an endo-psychic defect. As a compensatory function, the attempt is highly successful. The price paid however for such compensation is excessive. Gullibility and credulity are some of the excessive costs involved. The history narrated in this volume is ample evidence.

Certainly there must be several ways of dealing with this psychological phenomenon that plays such havoc with occult students. But it seems to me that the traditional occult way–at least in the West–is defective in some manner. Whoever one considers in the recent history of the Western secret tradition is almost always either an egotist of gigantic proportions or else an abject Uriah Heep! The Eastern method of the total subservience of the chela to the guru appears on the surface to be infinitely more effective. While this is clearly so, it is evident that such Eastern methods cannot be readily adopted to the Westerner.

Therefore, our magical tradition needs to be supplemented by techniques which either it had at one time and lost, or never possessed at all.

The best source for such assistance is to be found within the current psychological field. This is not to say that all psychologists and psychiatrists have mastered or resolved their own neurotic conflicts, or that all methods are equally satisfactory. But it can be safely asserted that its basic tools are well adapted for the resolution of this disturbing problem. That commonly found fantasy of many occult writers and students–of being in touch with Masters or inner plane Adepti–is so evidently neurotic, or even blatantly delusional, that most of those claiming it would have done better to have included some kind of psychotherapy in their early magical training. They would then have become familiar with the meaning and motive of the whole world of fantasy and dream with its manifest distortions, perversions and aberrations. At the very least, such therapy might have saved some from making utter fools of themselves and others from total destruction.

I have seen absolutely nothing in the past thirty years to deflect me from my primary conviction that psychotherapy, regardless of type of school, needs to be made a part of the curriculum of every Mystery School. Arguments that meditative techniques, astrological insights, and visionary experience lead in the direction of self-knowledge are true enough. I have no argument with these facts. But the subtle effects of ego inferiority, concealed as it is within the unconscious depths of the psyche, are so extensive and insidious that unless the student has a guru of first class quality, his meditations and insights and visions will become totally distorted without his even being aware that such his the case.

In conclusion, I would like to state that like *The Golden Dawn*, this book *My Rosicrucian Adventure* languished for nearly thirty years before the first edition was exhausted. In due course of time, extraordinary premiums were commanded by these books in the used book market, much to my consternation–for this was not as I expected or hoped.

Meanwhile, it must be added that for purely personal reasons I had relinquished my claim to the copyrights of these books, one of several motives being the ridiculous fear that the occult public would feel I had written these books solely for personal gain. In fact, this was overtly stated by the late Paul Foster Case–but fortunately in this instance, since we came to be friends, I was able to dispel the misinformation without any difficulty.

A few years ago, Llewellyn Publications obtained the copyrights of these and others of my early books to begin a vigorous program of republication. It would appear that now the time is ripe, the public is ready, and a new order of things is upon us. It resulted in my being asked to prepare a new Introduction to *My Rosicrucian Adventure* preparatory to another edition being placed on the book market.

Simultaneously, a number of events were occurring which caused me to postpone writing the Introduction for a short time. These events consisted of the publication, quite independently of Llewellyn Publications or myself, of some books which either corroborated my own personal viewpoint or else elaborated them with additional facts.

Two of these books are of enormous importance, while one of them is relatively insignificant. The publication of all three, however, justified the delay I had proposed before writing this Introduction. A more or less lengthy consideration of these books to elaborate the particular history narrated in the text of *My Rosicrucian Adventure* will be found in the Postscript to this volume, p. 141 *et seq*. It has been placed there so as not to interfere with the new student's possible understanding of these matters.

The general reader by then will have gained some perception of the total situation, and can pass on to reading the text itself of my experience in a Rosicrucian Order. I am quite certain that he will find himself reminiscing about similar experiences of his own, not necessarily with the Hermetic Order of the Golden Dawn, but with other occult fraternities, and he will understand that human nature is always human nature, occultism and mysticism notwithstanding. And if he has reached the age of tolerance and forbearance as I believe I now have, he will but nod his head and murmur, in effect, "That's the way things are!"

An Introduction to Aleister Crowley's
THE LAW IS FOR ALL
By Israel Regardie
Falcon Press, First Edition, 1985

In the year 1920, Aleister Crowley established his Abbey of Thelema in the village of Cefalu in Sicily. There he wrote his commentary on *The Book of the Law*. It is in many ways the most important and powerful document he ever penned. For the first time, he recorded with some degree of completeness his basic attitudes toward sex and love. He had never attempted anything comparable before. Here and there, it is true, were some sporadic excursions into the subject, but any comprehensive delineation of the doctrine of his heart, as it were, somehow always got sidetracked despite his extensive literary output.

I

In the book *Magick without Tears* (Phoenix: Falcon Press, 1983), he had made some significant but short remarks about the triad of sex, drugs and religion. His commentary is in reality a systematic elaboration on all three matters in addition to the topic of violence, which has only recently zoomed into the headlines throughout this country.

For example, so far as sex is concerned, Crowley rhapsodizes:

We of Thelema are not the slaves of Love. "Love under Will" is the Law. We refuse to regard Love as shameful and degrading, as a peril to body and soul. We refuse to accept it as the surrender of the divine to the animal; to us it is the means by which the animal may be made the Winged Sphinx which will bear man aloft to the House of the Gods.

Our current sexual attitudes, which he constantly attacked, are irrational. The Supreme Court of the United States has defined pornography in such a way that to write about sex and sexual acts is approved so long as the writing does not stimulate lascivious or sexual feelings. The writing must be kept subservient to the dictates of social significance and art—a fundamentally sex-negative outlook. Such a ruling is analogous to saying that it is legitimate for a writer to describe gourmet foods or fine cooking without stimulating the appetite or making one's mouth water, or that a writer may describe gourmet foods or fine cooking without stimulating the appetite or making one's mouth water, or that a writer may describe the beauty of the Greek isles and the clarity of sky and air, but only in such a way that no reader becomes imbued with the desire to travel there. None of this makes any sense. If a woman reads a fashion magazine describing new clothes without feeling moved to acquire a new wardrobe, then quite evidently the writing has failed to achieve an effect, and the magazine should go out of business.

A young contemporary writer, Mark Gerzon, wrote recently that the major characteristic of the young people's rebellion against the sexual values of adult society is perhaps the practically total rejection of tradition by many of his generation. He then adds that those of his generation are characterized by their psychological orientation, their need to be involved, and their awareness that the essence of life is human relations.

The acceptance of current social values, he feels, leads to emotional isolation. So it is of little wonder that many young people react to socially patterned sexual frustration with such vehemence. Even marriage, which society offers as the answer to their problems, comes under criticism. Marriage, as it is now, seems hardly the answer.

Regarding the next topic, drugs, Crowley sermonizes in his commentary:

> Therefore they [the puritanical slaves] fly to drink and drugs as to an anesthetic in the surgical operation of introspection.
>
> The craving for these things is caused by the internal misery which their use reveals to the slave-souls. If you are really free, you can take cocaine as simply as salt-water taffy. There is no better rough test of a soul than its attitude to drugs. If a man is simple, fearless, eager, he is all right; he will not become a slave. If he is afraid, he is already a slave. Let the whole world take opium, hashish, and the rest; those who are liable to abuse them were better dead.

This may or may not be valid reasoning. Marijuana and perhaps lysergic acid (LSD) may be taken without threat of physical addiction. The reasoning is hardly valid when heroin and morphine are concerned. The facts are too evident in the social debacle of today. Crowley himself struggled for several years toward the end of his life to free himself from addiction to heroin–unsuccessfully. It had originally been prescribed for him in 1919 by a physician for the treatment of his bronchial asthma. Much in the preceding passage has to be dismissed as fine sounding rhetoric, not fact, written during Crowley's own intoxication with heroin.

Again, compare this with some of Gerzon's thinking on the same topic. His book *The Whole World is Watching* (New York: Paperback Library, 1970) should be read as an adjunct to Crowley's commentary.

The current reaction to popular psychedelic drugs in the West suggests that the individual feels he was not aware of his life to the maximum before using these drugs. The cumulative effect of psychedelic exaltation is to feel more aware (i.e., more open and prone to perceive) of the beauty that is part of life. The common reaction is that the drug user realizes that, despite the luxury, the ease, and the convenience of modern culture, its members are missing much of the beauty and pleasure they could experience.

According to drug ideology, the inner, psychic world is made more sensitive, much like the senses. It is clear to the devotee that mental associations are liberated from the constraints imposed upon them by cultural patterns. Memories and feelings usually repressed are freed. The college generation uses drugs as tools for furthering self-analysis designed to eradicate the self-defeating engrams that have been left by mass society.

Religion, in the commentary, gets the following treatment by Crowley:

> There are to be no regular temples of Nuit and Hadit, for they are incommensurables and absolutes. Our religion, therefore, for the people, is the Cult of the Sun, who is our particular star of the Body of Nuit, from whom, in the strictest scientific sense, come this earth, a chilled spark of Him, and all our Light and Life. His vice-regent and representative in the animal kingdom is His cognate symbol the Phallus, representing Love and Liberty. Ra-Hoor-Khuit, like all true Gods, is therefore a Solar-Phallic deity...
>
> All those acts which excite the divine in man are proper to the rite of invocation.
>
> Religion, as understood by the vile Puritan, is the very opposite of all this. He–it–seems to wish to kill his–its–soul by forbidding every expression of it, and every practice which might awaken it to expression. To Hell with this Verbotenism!

> In particular, let me exhort all men and all women, for they are Stars! Heed well this holy verse!
>
> True Religion is intoxication, in a sense. We are told elsewhere to intoxicate the innermost, not the outermost; but I think that the word "wine" should be taken in its widest sense as meaning that which brings out the soul. Climate, soil and race change conditions; each man or woman must find and choose the fit intoxication. Thus hashish in one or other of its forms seems to suit the Moslem, to go with dry heat; opium is right for the Mongol; whiskey for the dour temperament and damp cold climate of the Scot...Religious ecstasy is necessary to man's soul. Where this is attained by mystical practices, directly, as it should be, people need no substitute...

He could have added that the clear vodka is ideal for the manic-depressive Russian in his icy cold climate, and that rum is appropriate for the Caribbean and the Polynesian areas.

That Crowley is writing directly for the young people of today is self-evident. The commentary is to be contrasted with Gerzon's criticism of religion as practiced in America today.

Religion in American society, Gerzon feels, has come to appear so hypocritical that young people feel they can gain more by turning to the religions of other cultures. The God presented to this generation by adult society is a shallow one. It is a God donated to the parents by their parents before them who had been raised in nineteenth-century fundamentalism. But the God this generation's parents were given in their childhood didn't fit in post-World War II American society. Most parents were unable to reject the religious beliefs of their childhood, but somehow could manage to adapt their social behavior to the secular consumption-and-prestige oriented culture of the 1950s and 1960s. This generation saw and rejected the ambivalence of the religious values of adult society exemplified in their parents.

And so far as violence is concerned, Crowley vividly expresses his point of view thus:

> Fight! Fight like gentlemen, without malice, because fighting is the best game in the world, and love the second best! Don't slander your enemy, as the newspapers would have you do; just kill him, and then bury him with honour. Don't keep crying "Foul" like a fifth-rate pugilist. Don't boast! Don't squeal. If you're down, get up and hit him again! Fights of that sort make fast friends.

Would that Crowley had been able to fight in this way–instead of merely preaching it!

Throughout the second chapter of the commentary, and only occasionally in the third, is the recurrent theme, a chorus, as it were, of "the Christians to the Lions." He is here expressing his thoroughgoing contempt for Christianity in all its forms, a contempt which had its origins in his early revolt against the excessive fundamentalism of the Plymouth Brethren, the religion of his parents. "My primary objection to Christianity," he writes here, "is 'gentle Jesus, meek and mild' the pacifist, the conscientious objector, the Tolstoyan, the passive resister."

Every now and again, he begrudgingly strives to make an exception of the Catholics in Latin countries, feeling that they were essentially pagan in outlook, only to revoke it a few paragraphs later. All Protestants of every denomination come within the jurisdiction of his condemnation to the lions. The Jews are also condemned roundly, though in one paragraph he confines his condemnation to Jews living in America. Apparently, they are not bellicose enough to come up to his standards. He did not live long enough to come up to his standards. He did not live long enough to see a handful of Israelis take on the surrounding Arab nations who numbered millions. Though *Liber Legis* does mildly castigate the Moslems. Crowley still retains his profound admiration for the so-called manliness of the Arab, his courage and ferocity. It may be that his homosexual experiences in the Sahara influenced profoundly his attitude toward them.

There is also some magnificent if wild humor in these pages. Whether it is intentional or inadvertent is hard to judge from the nature of the remarks. But his panagyric about Woman–which would in part please the current feminist movement, and horrify them at the same time–is so outrageously funny as well as rhetorical, that it should become a classic of the English language to be employed whenever the "fair sex" needs mentioning. The first of these reads:

> Hence, the pretence that a woman is "pure," modest, delicate, aesthetically beautiful and morally exalted, ethereal and unfleshly, though in fact they know her to be lascivious, shameless, coarse, ill-shapen, unscrupulous, nauseatingly bestial both physically and mentally. The advertisements of "dress-shields," perfumes, cosmetics, anti-sweat preparations, and "beauty treatments" reveal woman's nature as seen by the clear eyes of those who would lose money if they misjudged her; and they are loathsomely revolting to read. Her mental and moral characteristics are those of the parrot and the monkey. Her physiology and pathology are hideously disgusting, a sickening slime of uncleanliness.
>
> Her virgin life is a sick ape's, her sexual life a drunken sow's, her mother life all bulging filmy and sagging udders.

This is countered by:

> Not only art thou Woman, sworn to a purpose not thine own; thou art thyself a star, and in thyself a purpose to thyself. Not only mother of men art thou, or whore to men; serf to their need of Life and Love, not sharing their Light and Liberty; nay, though art Mother and Whore for thine own pleasure; the Word I say to Man I say to thee no less: Do what thou wilt shall be the whole of the Law!...
>
> There is a Cry in an unknown tongue, it resounds through the Temple of the Universe; in its one Word is Death and Ecstasy, and the title of honour, o thou, to Thyself High Priestess, Prophetess, Empress, to Thyself the Goddess whose Name means Mother and Whore!

However–and this is the most important issue–anybody who hitherto had entertained any doubts or misconceptions as to what Aleister Crowley stood for concerning these topics and life itself, must now find here some absolute clarification. If for no other reason than the above, his commentary expounding his life philosophy represents a high-water mark in Crowley's literary and spiritual career.

It would be wise to remember that Crowley reached his majority in the *fin-de-siecle* when some very good minds as well as many dilettantes were attacking the establishment in Great Britain. There it was represented by Queen Victoria, whom many regarded as the staid and last bulwark of Christian morality and order.

There was as yet no psychoanalytic literature to reveal what volcanic force and fire burned in man's unconscious deeps. Freud had begun hesitantly and falteringly to write in 1985, and then only in German. It took many years for his explosive and shattering ideas to filter down through the different European languages, including English, and reach the intelligentsia.

By then, Sir Richard Burton had translated *The Arabian Nights*. It included some erudite footnotes together with a lengthy appendix mostly about the geography and distribution of homosexual practices. In addition, there were some few other enterprising and original souls represented by the *Yellow Book* and similar literary ventures.

There was, however, no clear delineation or final formulation of a general creed of sexual liberation, save for the idealistic writing of a very few writers. Even in the year 1904 when *The Book of the Law* came to be written down, Europe and America were still bound up in the heavy iron chains of Judeo-Christian morality. God was not dead–yet, though Nietzsche had tried his utmost to inter him. Nor had any great majority of that generation made any concerted move to scrap the existent moral and social systems. It is true that just prior to World War II there was a widespread pacifist movement. However, it ended almost wholly with the German invasion of Poland and the Japanese aerial assault on Pearl Harbor. That generation, however, was pacifist only, not having yet come to formulate any concept of a total rejection of *all* of society, including its roots and foundations.

It has only been in recent years, with the rise of this current generation–white as well as black–descendants of the Beat generation, that contemporary standards have been challenged successfully and are in danger of being overthrown. *The Sexual Revolution* and other timely and important books written by Wilhelm Reich in the 1930s and early 1940s, obviously have had a great deal to do with this challenge. In fact, he was a pioneer where this great social work is concerned, and is being widely read today.

Aldous Huxley perhaps leads off the contemporary parade with his little book, *Doors of Perception*, written after his mescaline experience. That book and that experience demonstrated to the world at large that fixed and conventional attitudes toward general living were arbitrary and could be transcended in a sensory and mind-expanding experience, initiated by certain drugs. Many others, it is true, had written of this long before Huxley's time and his book. De Quincey, Ludlow, Baudelaire, and many others had experimented with psychedelic drugs. (See *The Marijuana Papers*, edited by David Solomon; New York: Signet Books, 1966.) But none of these people seem to have made the considerable impact on the general public that Huxley achieved.

I am almost of the opinion that it was not until Leary, Alpert and Metzner overtly began to experiment with psychedelic drugs, thus earning their expulsion from Harvard University in the 1960s, that an insidiously quiet but overwhelmingly powerful movement was initiated, which would spread across not merely the United States but all over Europe and in fact the whole world. While we need not be in accord with the overfacile slogan, "Turn on, tune in, drop out," nevertheless, Leary deserves great commendation for his heroic efforts to state the unpopular facts regarding the sacramental usage of drugs, regardless of what his motives may or may not have been.

More closely than anybody else, he seems to have approached the attitudes of Aleister Crowley almost exactly. I made some comparisons of these not too long ago in *Roll Away the Stone* (St. Paul, Minnesota: Llewellyn Publications, 1969). In fact, while reading Leary's interview with one of the editors of *Playboy* magazine some years ago, it seemed almost possible to hear the overtones of Crowley speaking a half-century previously. For it was in that interview that Leary expounded not only the possibility of the transcendental experience in the usage of marijuana, etc., but its tendency also to liberate sexual drives and feelings, which was the reason, so he felt, for the opposition by the establishment.

In this I am not to be construed as condoning the *indiscriminate* usage of drugs–certainly not those labeled "hard" narcotics. These are definitely not for young people to play with, nor adults, either, for that matter. Intelligent familiarity with usage, purpose and pharmaco-dynamics of the psychedelic agents is still required for those old enough to use them seriously. Otherwise there may be an increasingly large harvest of psychotic breakdowns–heavy enough at this writing–due to spontaneous eruptions from an unconscious psyche whose thresholds have been recklessly opened up by ignorant tampering. The dangers are real enough, and need to be evaluated, and the psychological stability of the users estimated. With such knowledge and with proper (that is, trained or professional) supervision, experiments can be carried on with a view of determining how deeper self-knowledge and perception may be possible. I do not deny that there have been many disasters due to the contemporary use of drugs. The doubters should visit any mental hospital. I am sure that there must be thousands of ill-advised users who have fallen heir to psychic disaster. There are bound to be many who, for one reason or another, have become victims of this rebellion. This is the price that unfortunately does have to be paid.

If marijuana and lysergic acid, with its attendant disasters, are the means of opening a whole new generation to the "cult of the occult," as Rollo May once termed it, then that really is a very small price to pay. I take the viewpoint of Crowley here. If some are overcome and die or are killed, then they are merely through for this incarnation and free to resume the struggle for freedom in the next life. One has to view man's progress not merely in the light of the here and now, which is important enough, but also *sub species aeternitatis*.

> *Never the spirit was born,*
>   *The spirit shall cease to be never.*
> *Never was time it was not,*
>   *End and beginning are dreams.*
> *Birthless and deathless and changeless*
>   *Remaineth the spirit for ever;*
> *Death hath not touched it at all,*
> *Dead though the house of it seems!*
>   –Sir Edwin Arnold
>   *The Song Celestial*

It is worthwhile to quote directly from *The Whole World Is Watching*, for the young author has something most important to add in this connection:

Marijuana was not invented in 1965. It is ancient. Even in America it has been used for decades in urban subcultures and in rural areas where it grows wild. The only thing that is new is the extent of alienation in white, middle-class, educated young people and their consequent openness to the values of pot-smoking. Much of the recent severe criticism of marijuana is the result not of new and more accurate research but of the spread of its use into "respectable" society…

Unaware of the nature of youth culture, most adults consider the popularity of marijuana as ephemeral as that of a new dance. "Oh, those kids!" an old lady exclaimed to me. "It's a new dance or a new singing group every few months. And now drugs too. The fads pass, but some of them are dangerous." This lady felt that drugs were something that just caught kids' fancies. Complacent adults sit back and wait for pot to go out like the hula hoop.

What is frightening is how poorly these adults read the signs of their own culture. Rather than being a passing breeze (or smoke fume), marijuana is an element of youth culture that has taken root in the soil of this generation's psychological alienation. The plant will not be uprooted unless the deep roots of discontent are recognized. Drug usage will not diminish as long as the alienation in youth culture grows.

Before leaving this topic of drugs, attention ought to be directed to some observations of Dr. Don Wilson who, for three years, served as a prison psychologist at Fort Leavenworth. He wrote the popular book, *My Six Convicts*, as a result of that experience, but some of his shrewd observations and conclusions seem to have been entirely overlooked during the past two decades. For example, he wrote: "The physical damage done by phenobarbital compounds is more insidious and extensive than that of the dangerous drugs under discussion." And so far as marijuana addiction is concerned, he wrote as long ago as 1952:

The upper- and middle-class users in medicine, business, law, engineering, teaching and the theater use discretion, watch their health, show none of the symptoms of addiction, and are almost never detected or apprehended. Statements regarding this high-class user are based on individual observation, while researches made on masses are heavily weighted with people from the wrong side of the tracks who are maladjusted, maladroit and inadequate in the face of life and pressure.

It is in the nature of things that vast movements in one direction are following by a movement in its direct opposite. In fact, we already see the beginning of what may be an extensive backlash against drug usage, the youth revolt, college demonstrations, and black violence. It may almost seem as if most of the modern progressive movements will be negated and replaced by the most conservative trends. It is also in the nature of things that the backlash will be succeeded by its opposite. In due time, however, what little progress was involved in these pendulum swings will become apparent. But this may not be clarified for some hundreds of years, at least until the new Aeon really gets under way. We are merely in the opening stages of this Age of Aquarius, and there is likely to be a great deal of instability until the essential characteristics of the Age assert themselves.

More and more evidence presents itself to indicate an ever-widening alienation between conventional society, i.e., the establishment, and the younger generation. The better the education of the latter, the wider seems the alienation. In other words, this generation does not fit into society as we know it. Their aims, ideals and standards bear little relation to those widely accepted. To be alienated, states Gerzon, certainly does not imply that one has to be sitting on the curb, barefoot, somewhere on the Sunset Strip, with a beard on one's face, beads around the neck, and a joint hanging from the corner of the mouth. To be alienated means to be dissatisfied with the kind of personality and life experience that our culture recognizes and expects. The number of possibly alienated young people far exceeds the estimates behind which adult society hides from the truth.

It is for them, then, that Crowley wrote his commentary. They are the early representatives of the Aquarian Age, the Aeon of the new crowned and conquering child Horus, the Lord of the New Aeon. They are the love children who are violent and militant and epicene—simultaneously. One of the commonest of current jokes relates to the difference between the two sexes becoming so flimsy as to render recognition at first sight almost impossible. A couple of youngsters go to a gynecologist. They both have long hair, smooth, girlish skin and faces, and wear fringed leather jackets and worn blue jeans. The doctor, not wishing to embarrass them by asking which one of the two was the girl in need of attention, asks instead, "Which of you has the menstrual cycle?" They both answer, perplexed, "Oh,–we drive Hondas!"

One of Crowley's most frequently expressed ideas was that as the years progress into this new age, more and more people will come into incarnation with bisexual characteristics. They will be epicene. I never expected to see this statement corroborated as early as it has been.

For example, homosexuals who previously had kept themselves well concealed from public view are now emerging in full sight. I am thinking specifically of Los Angeles where a gay liberation group is overtly declaring itself, but this is the case elsewhere too. There have been several mass demonstrations, and announcements are regularly publicized naming their meetings for all to see and attend. Harassment from police authorities still exists but is diminishing, and in due course must cease altogether. It is more than likely that their numbers will grow considerably as others, who previously were cautious and frightened, come out of hiding. Current laws relative to homosexuality will have to be modified or repealed as they have already been in Great Britain.

Female homosexuals, lesbians, are also undergoing a similar metamorphosis. Practically the entire front page of one section of the *Sunday Times* in Los Angeles was recently given over to a frank discussion of lesbians and their characteristics and problems in modern society. What is particularly interesting in this connection is the developing insistence that the sexual deviate is not sick, or no more sick than the average heterosexual in our society. Those of us who retain a static psychoanalytic orientation relative to homosexuality, male or female, were all too prone to attribute homosexuality to basic dynamic factors and conflicts in childhood. This was my point of view expressed in *The Eye in the Triangle*, published by Llewellyn Publications in 1970 but begun around 1965. Less and less credibility is to be attached to this attitude today and I think the change is a healthy one.

"Ye are against the people, O my chosen." The common man is the advocate of commonness. A new game has recently been coined for this specimen of humanity. Roger Price has written a new book entitled *The Great Roob Revolution* (New York: Random House, 1970).

The author paints a picture of the Roobs–mass men, the *homo normalis* so contemptuously named by Reich–having come into their own as a dynamic social force. Since their numbers are overwhelming and they are enjoying affluence for the first time, they are attempting to impose still further their ideas and attitudes upon the total population. Mass taste rules the world.

If this is indeed the case, then evidently in these traditional stages of the New Aeon a great deal of public ferment and disorder is certain, at least in the early years. For *The Book of the Law*, as quoted above, is adamantly against the rule of mass man. We shall witness many disturbances in the years to come as their bad taste in social organization, religion and politics gradually increases and then diminishes.

The mid-fifties were characterized by theories and feelings that a revolution in social thinking was overdue. Apparently, however, no one could work up enough of a head of steam to get things moving. But the theoretical concepts were there. For example, I am thinking of one fine psychological writer in particular, the late Robert Lindner. He was the author of *Prescription for Rebellion* which almost made the mark, though I suspect the time was not yet ripe for the emergence of a movement to devise widespread change of patterns of thought and behavior. Attention needs to be redirected to it, however, because there are some saving principles enunciated there.

It was basic to his thinking that all Western society is "neurotic" since Western man lives only according to taboos, myths, legends–beliefs without foundation in fact. Yet the average psychiatrist, Lindner complained, tries to "adjust" his patients to placid acceptance of a maladjusted society. This procedure has caused many to condemn psychological practice as a "quack religion." And so it is, according to Lindner, whenever it offers the individual no more than resubmergence in mass man. If psychological science is sound, then in order to save Western man, our fundamental behavior and basic beliefs must be made to yield to the efforts of informed rebels. It has taken several years for the "informed rebels" to surface and make their influence felt.

As I understand it from frequent discussions with patients from the young hip generation, many of them turned on to the new sexual, social and political attitudes through their initial use of marijuana. However much some adults may be shocked and horrified by this revelation, it is more than clear that the psychedelic drugs have to take prime place as factors responsible for the overturning of contemporary moral, religious and social standards, for the transvaluation of values. This is the prelude to an eventual development of a radically new code of behavior and therefore a radically new type of society, as indicated by *The Book of the Law*.

Who could have foreseen in 1904 that the world was about to take a radical turn in the direction of chaos and disaster? It seems that the rationalists then were absolutely convinced that more education, more commerce, more science, more of everything was on its way; and that these would initiate the golden age of peace, security and universal brotherhood.

For example, in *This Fabulous Century* (New York: Time Life Books, 1970) were several statements typifying the above attitude. At the opening of the twentieth century, Mark Hanna of Ohio said "Furnaces are glowing, spindles are singing their song. Happiness comes to us all with prosperity."

And the Rev. Newell Dwight Hillis of Brooklyn wrote, "Laws are becoming more just, rulers humane; music is becoming sweeter and books wiser."

Those of us who knew the League of Nations, and who believed in its present-day successor the United Nations, had high hopes initially that here were the answers to many age-old problems and that nations would not go to war any more. They would lay down their armaments and turn them into pruning hooks and the lion would lie down with the lamb. How wrong we were! And how unaware of the fundamentally biological facts of human nature, as indicated in *African Genesis*, for instance. But *The Book of Law* and Aleister Crowley correctly assessed the situation as no one else may level at Crowley, we have to come to terms with the total revolution predicted by that book as early as 1904. This is Crowley's justification. And this is the final warrant demanding that at least he be given a fair hearing.

In *Magick without Tears*, Crowley discussed his serial publication *The Equinox* and his motives for publishing it. One of his remarks is fascinating: "They [the Secret Chiefs of the Order]...were agreed on measures calculated to assure the survival of the Wisdom worth saving until the time, perhaps three hundred or six hundred years later, when a new current should revive the shattered thought of mankind."

In the last chapter of *The Eye in The Triangle*, I had interpreted one verse in *Liber Legis* to imply that a holocaust or a vast natural cataclysm was in the offing, to occur sometime during the 1980s, when Pluto moves into Scorpio. Whatever this event may turn out to be, it could hold up the wheels of progress for some considerable time, perhaps for as long as Crowley has predicted above.

Somewhere around 1990, there will be a great conjunction of planets in the heavens that augur very little good for anybody. Neptune, Uranus, Saturn, Mars, Mercury, Venus, the Sun and the Moon will be in conjunction in the sign of Capricorn, around January-February, 1990. At the same time, Jupiter will be in square aspect to the sign Libra. China is Libra-ruled according to astrologers, and Africa is ruled by Capricorn. Just what the significance of the above conjunction is, most astrologers will not say; that would be sticking their necks out entirely too far. But if this conjunction and the previous predictions are tied together, perhaps some vague intimation may be obtained of what kind of Dark Age lies ahead.

It may also serve to explain what Crowley referred to as "a new current...[to] revive the shattered thought of mankind."

II

In order to render this most important volume as complete as possible, I have taken certain liberties which perhaps were not contemplated by Crowley in the writing of it. For example, I have included the Stele of Revealing primarily because there are so many references to it that the student approaching this matter for the first time may not understand what is referred to. Of course, he could consult either *The Equinox*, Vol. I, No. 10, or *The Equinox of the Gods* where this Stele is reproduced. But that would entail some inconvenience which can be obviated by simply reproducing it here.

Moreover, since the last chapter of *The Book of Law* commands, "Paste the sheets from right to left and from top to bottom: then behold!," with the interference that there is a mystery concealed within the holograph manuscript, I have decided to conform to its dictates. I have, therefore, included Crowley's reproduction of the holograph pages conforming to the above, taken from *The Equinox*, Vol. I, No 10, on the supposition that it will facilitate study of the original.

Again, though *The Book of Law* is given *in toto* in the commentary, it is broken up into sections that are specifically commented upon. I have decided to reproduce the entire book itself as it was printed in *The Equinox*, Vol. I, No. 9, as a preliminary to the rest. This too may prove to be useful.

The distribution of Crowley's commentaries is interesting. He originally wrote a brief commentary which was published in *The Equinox*, Vol. I, No. 7. In his Extenuation, he reproduced the brief commentary to chapters two and three and labeled it the "old comment" to precede his later remarks, which he called the "new comment." Only in chapter one has he omitted the old comment, and his new remarks are reproduced without the adjective "new" in the heading. New students would need to consult the mentioned volume of *The Equinox* in order to read what the old comment to chapter one stated. Again, in order to obviate the necessity for consulting other books, I have taken the liberty of following Crowley's example in the last two chapters of this volume, by breaking up the comment in *The Equinox* into its appropriate parts, labeling it as the "old comment," and following it immediately by what I have now called the "new comment." Nothing is changed in the wording of the text. It is simply an inclusion which I believe to be a logical necessity. It is one which renders easier the study of this book.

In presenting Crowley's *Extenuation* to the general public, I should mention that I have not dared to meddle with the text, except to standardize somewhat spelling, punctuation and capitalization. I have wanted to, I must admit. In many places I have thought it redundant, verbose and occasionally mystifying. In fact, some years ago my original impression was that it included some superb prose, a large number of "purple passages," and a vast amount of just plain rhetoric.

For example, a "purple passage" typical of many is the following:

> The supreme and absolute injunction, the crux of your knightly oath, is that you lay your lance in rest to the glory of your Lady, the Queen of the Stars, Nuit. Your knighthood depends on your refusal to fight in any lesser cause. This is what distinguishes you from the brigand and the bully. You give your life on her altar. You make yourself worthy of Her by your readiness to fight at any time, in any place, with any weapon, and at any

odds. For Her for Whom you came, of Whom you are, to Whom you go, your life is no more and no less than one continuous sacrament. You have no word but her praise, no thought but love of Her. You have only one cry, of inarticulate ecstasy, and intense spasm, possession of Her, and Death, to Her. You have no act but the priest's gesture that makes your body Hers...

And as for rhetoric, there is a great deal of it, characterized by such sentences as:

> Alas! it is I the Beast that roared that Word so loud, and wakened Beauty.
>
> Your tricks, your drowsy drugs, your life, your hypnotic passes–they will not serve you.
>
> Make up your minds to be free men, fearless as I, fit mates for women no less free and fearless!
>
> For I, the Beast, am come; an end to the evils of old, to the duping and clubbing of abject and ailing animals, degraded to that shameful state to serve that shameful pleasure.
>
> The essence of my Word is to declare Woman to be Herself, of, to and for, Herself; and I give this one irresistible Weapon, the expression of Herself and Her will through sex, to Her on precisely the same terms as to a man.

Fortunately, good prose runs throughout the whole book. There is no special need to highlight any particular paragraph or passage. The reader can open the book at any page at random to find some splendid writing.

Regardless of my feelings in this matter, and no matter how I personally may feel about *The Book of the Law* or Aleister Crowley, both should be permitted to speak for themselves.

The sole substantive editing that I have confined myself to, therefore, is merely to clarify the topic of several dates, using the common method rather than referring all events back to the date of *The Book of the Law*, in 1904. I have removed some of his Qabalistic renderings of both the Greek and Hebrew alphabets to an appendix. This makes for easier reading.

Finally, I have to call attention to Crowley's selection of a title for this book: *An Extenuation of the Book of Law*. I feel this is a rather clumsy title which may have little to say to most readers. I have accordingly deleted it and substituted a phrase taken from the text itself, *The Book of Law*. Admittedly this presumption may not convey much more–certainly not that it is a commentary at great length on the Law–but at least it is simpler and may intrigue the casual reader enough to demand that he open the book and glance at its contents.

How and why *The Book of the Law* came to be written has been amply described by Crowley himself both in *The Temple of Solomon the King*, a serial biography running through the various numbers of *The Equinox* (1909-1914), and in *The Equinox of the Gods*, published in 1936 by the O.T.O. in England. Since that time, Crowley's own autobiography–also written in the Cefalu period–has appeared (New York: Hill and Wang, 1970). Some of the details are amplified in this commentary to considerable advantage for all readers.

An Introduction to Robert Anton Wilson's
PROMETHEUS RISING
By Israel Regardie
New Falcon Publications, First Edition, 2017

The ability to create a synthesis of diverse points of view, scientific and social and philosophical, is a rare gift. Not many are there who dare even to attempt such a task.

Imagine anyone trying to make sense of an amalgam of Timothy Leary's eight neurological circuits, Gurdjieff's self-observation exercises, Korzybski's general semantics, Aleister Crowley's magical theorems, the several disciplines of Yoga, Christian Science, relativity and modern quantum mechanics, and many other approaches to understanding the world around us! A man is required with an almost encyclopedic education, an incredibly flexible mind, insights as sharp as those whom he is trying to synthesize and *mirabile dictu*, a wonderful sense of humor.

For several years—ever since I first became familiar with the writings of Robert Anton Wilson—I have been struck with his ever-present sense of bubbling humor and the wide scope of his intellectual interests. Once I was even so presumptuous as to warn him in a letter that his humor was much too good to waste on the hoi polloi who, generally speaking, would not understand it and might even resent it. However this effervescent lightness of heart became even more apparent in *The Cosmic Trigger* and more latterly in the trilogy of *Schrödinger's Cat*. I have sometimes wondered whether his extraordinarily wide range of intellectual roving is too extensive and therefore perplexing to the average reader. Be that as it may, the humor and synthesis are even more marked in this brilliant ambitious piece of writing, *Prometheus Rising*.

Even if your reading has already made you familiar with some of the concepts employed by Wilson in this book, nonetheless his elucidation even of the simplest, the most basic, is illuminating. At this moment, I am referring to the "imprint" theory which he makes considerable use of. Much of the same is true of his references to and explanation of Leary's eight neurological circuits. We become familiar with them all over again, as if they had not been introduced to us before.

Moreover, I love the subtle and almost invisible use of mystical dogma that permeates all his writings. For example, consider the opening of Chapter Six. It quotes a particularly meaningful sentence from William S. Burroughs. There is no mention—nor need there be—of any anterior teaching regarding this Law of Three, as it may be called. But one doctrine that emanated from a mediaeval mystical school philosophizes that there are always two contending forces—for the sake of convenience labelled Severity and Mildness—with a third that always reconciles them. It is paramount to this doctrine, which has been stated and stated again in a dozen or more different ways throughout the centuries, culminating finally in the idea enunciated by Burroughs and, of course, used by Wilson.

There are dozens of similar seeds of wisdom sown throughout *Prometheus Rising* that are bound to have a seminal effect wherever and whenever the book is read. This is one of the many virtues of Wilson's book; it will leave its mark on all those who read it—and those seeds will surely take root and bloom in the most unlikely minds—as well as in the most prosaic. Tarot advocates will find the most unusual and illuminating interpretations of some of their favorite cards when he falls back on the basic neural circuits. I found them all illuminating as providing a new viewpoint which had to be integrated into my general view of such matters.

The only area where I was reluctantly inclined to be at odds with Wilson was in what I considered to be his addition to a Utopia—which he eloquently enough expresses as "the birth pangs of a cosmic Prometheus rising out of the long nightmare of domesticated primate history." The history of mankind is also the history of one Utopia after another, being enunciated with enthusiasm and vigor, calling upon all the facts of faith and science (as they existed at that moment in space-time) to corroborate the fantasy. A decade or maybe a century elapse—and the fantasy is no more. The Utopia has gone down the drain to join all the other Utopias of earlier primates. However, I sincerely hope that Wilson is *right* in this case.

Now I am not unmindful of the fact that the Utopia of which Wilson speaks, echoing many of the best scientific and philosophic minds of our day, is a distinct possibility at *some time*, but that it could occur within the next decade seems rather improbable to me. It seems improbable of course only in terms of the current state of world enlightenment, or lack of it, and because it implies a "miracle" occurring in vast numbers of living primates simultaneously—whatever semantic theories are involved in the meaning of the word "simultaneously."

Anyway, this is a minor point considering the seminal brilliance of the greater part of this enlightening book.

In a previously written book, Wilson wrote that in "1964, Dr. John S. Bell published a demonstration that still has the physicists reeling. What Bell seemed to prove was that quantum effects are 'non-local' in Bohm's sense; that is, they are not just here or there, but both. What this apparently means is that space and time are only real to our mammalian sense organs; they are not *really* real."

This writing reminds me so much of the Hindu concept of Indra's Net. The latter is sometimes described as being a great net extending throughout the whole universe, vertically to represent time, horizontally to represent space. At each point where the threads of this Indra's net cross one another is a diamond or a crystal bead, the symbol of a single existence. Each crystal bead reflects on its shining surface not only every other bead in the whole net of Indra but every single reflection of every reflection of every other bead upon each individual bead—countless, endless reflections of one another. We could also liken it to a single candle being placed in the centre of a large hall. Around this hall tens of mirrors are arranged in such a manner that, when the candle was lit, one saw not only its reflection in each individual mirror, but also the reflections of the reflections in every other mirror repeated *ad infinitum*.

One of the several virtues of *Prometheus Rising* is that Wilson using Leary's neurological circuits believes that a new philosophical paradigm is about due. In reality, this is really Wilson's answer to my proposed criticism of his Utopian fantasy. It may not be within a decade that we shall realized whether it is true or false. But that is not important. What is clear is that thanks to the insights of many modern thinkers, major new intellectual findings do not come solely from the slow drip and grind of tiny new discoveries, or from new theories simply being added to our present armamentarium of time-honoured truisms. Rather, quantum leaps in outlook *a la* Teilhard de Chardin, occur with a fantastic jump to a new horizon or level of perception. This insight usually comes from a revolutionary overview which realigns or transforms former thinking into a new and more enlightening frame of reference.

This dovetails with his equally fascinating thesis that everything alive is really *alive* in the fullest and most dynamic sense of the word. It twitches, searches, throbs, organizes and seems aware of an upward movement. Twitches seems almost the right word, recalling to mind the myoclonisms of Wilhelm Reich's vegetotherapy which, at some time, are infinitely disturbing to the patient on the couch who, because of them, feels he is falling apart, being shattered into a thousand pieces. He isn't really. It is as though the organism were gathering itself together for an upward or forward leap into the unknown, to a higher order of looking at things.

The transition to a higher order of functioning—or hooking on to a higher neural circuit—is often accompanied by considerable anxiety or a turbulence in personal life which seems as if the organism were falling apart or breaking up. This phenomenon of instability is really the way that every living organism—societies, human primates, chemical solutions, etc.—shakes itself, as it were, by myoclonism or similar convulsions into new combinations and permutations for higher and new levels of development. So perhaps the space-time Utopia of a new area of primate exploration has some validity after all, as indicating that the more vigorous the disturbance or myoclonism the greater the quantum jump into a higher neurological circuit. This is one reason why I firmly believe that the transition to the next spiral will not be smooth nor without much suffering and chaos.

All of which suggest, with Wilson and Leary, that the brain is considerably more sophisticated than any of us previously had imagined. It is quite possible that it operates in dimensions so beyond the lower neural circuitry that it occasionally "throws us a bone" every day so that we can continue to function in the make-believe world of everyday status quo. In the meantime, it is a multidimensional structure at ease in far more than the narrow primate world we have been programmed to live in. It may interpret waves and frequencies from other dimensions, realms of "light", of meaningful unrestricted patterned reality—that are here and now—and which transcend our present myopic tunnel realities of our rigid perceptions and conceptualizations of space and time.

If so, then the title of this book *Prometheus Rising* is representative of more than a catchy title to a profound fascination book. It becomes a title, instead, to the very attempt which we are now making to reach beyond ourselves with a quantum leap into a new world which has been envisaged only by a very few. Wilson is one of this group who are preparing themselves and if we allow them, the rest of us, to take our place in the New Aeon.

I will close with a quote from Wilson, "We are all giants, raised by pygmies, who have learned to walk with a perpetual mental coach. Unleashing our full stature—our total brain power—is what this book is all about."

Phoenix, Arizona
July 1983

An Introduction to
THE COMPLETE GOLDEN DAWN SYSTEM OF MAGIC
History of the Golden Dawn - The Early Years
by Israel Regardie[1]
New Falcon Publications, Fifth Revised Limited Edition, 2013

"The Order of the Golden Dawn," narrates the history lecture of that Order, "is an Hermetic Society whose members are taught the principles of Occult Science and the Magic of Hermes. During the early part of the second half of last century, several eminent Adepti and Chiefs of the Order in France and England died, and their death caused a temporary dormant condition of Temple work.

"Prominent among the Adepti of our Order and of public renown, were Eliphas Levi the greatest of modern French magi: Ragon, the author of several books of occult lore; Kenneth M. Mackenzie, author of the famous and learned Masonic Encyclopaedia, and Frederick Hockley possessed of the power of vision in the crystal, and whose manuscripts are highly esteemed. These and other contemporary Adepti of this Order received their knowledge and power from predecessors of equal and even of greater eminence. They received indeed and have

---

[1] Originally published in *My Rosicrucian Adventure*, (1936) which was revised and republished by New Falcon Publications, First Edition 2017.

handed down to us their doctrine and system of Theosophy and Hermetic Science and the higher Alchemy from a long series of practised investigators whose origin is traced to the Fratres Roseae Crucis of Germany, which association was founded by one Christian Rosenkreutz about the year 1398 A.D....

"The Rosicrucian revival of Mysticism was but a new development of the vastly older wisdom of the Qabalistic Rabbis and of that very ancient secret knowledge, the Magic of the Egyptians, in which the Hebrew Pentateuch tells you that Moses, the founder of the Jewish system was 'learned', in which he had been initiated." In a slender but highly informative booklet entitled *Data of the History of the Rosicrucians* published in 1916 by the late Dr. William Wynn Westcott, we find the following brief statement: "In 1887 by permission of S.D.A. [Anna Sprengel] a continental Rosicrucian Adept, the Isis-Urania Temple of Hermetic Students of the G.D. was formed to give instruction in the mediaeval Occult sciences. Fratres M.E.V. [William Robert Woodman] with S.A. [Dr. Wynn Westcott] and S.R.M.D. [S.L. MacGregor Mathers] became the chiefs, and the latter wrote the rituals in modern English from old Rosicrucian mss. (the property of S.A.) supplemented by his own literary researches."

In these two statements is narrated the beginning of the Hermetic Order of the Golden Dawn—an organisation which has exerted a greater influence on the development of Occultism since its revival in the last quarter of the 19th century than most people can realise. There can be little or no doubt that the Golden Dawn is, or rather was until very recently, the sole depository of magical knowledge, the only Occult Order of any real worth that the West in our time has known, and a great many other occult organisations owe what little magical knowledge is theirs to leakages issuing from that Order and from it renegade members.

The membership of the Golden Dawn was recruited from every circle, and it was represented by dignified professions as well as by all the arts and sciences, to make but little mention of the trades and business occupations. It included physicians, psychologists, clergymen, artists and philosophers; and normal men and women, humble and unknown, from every walk of life have drawn inspiration from its font of wisdom, and undoubtedly many would be happy to recognise and admit the enormous debt they owe to it.

As an organisation, it preferred always to shroud itself in an impenetrable cloak of mystery. Its teaching and methods of instruction were stringently guarded by various penalties attached to the most awe-inspiring obligations in order to ensure that secrecy. So well have these obligations with but one or two exceptions been kept that the general public knows next to nothing about the Order, its teaching, or the extent and nature of its membership. Though this book will touch upon the teaching of the Golden Dawn, concerning its membership as a whole the writer will have nothing to say, except perhaps to repeat what may already be more or less well-known. For instance, it is common knowledge that W.B. Yeats, Arthur Machen and, if rumour may be trusted, the late Arnold Bennett were at one time among its members, together with a good many other writers and artists.

With regard to the names given in Dr. Westcott's statement it is necessary that we bestow to them some little attention in order to unravel, so far as may be possible, the almost inextricable confusion which has characterised every previous effort to detail the history of the Order. M.E.V. was the motto chosen by Dr. William Robert Woodman, an eminent Freemason of the last century. Sapere Aude and Non Omnis Moriar were the two mottos used by Dr. Wescott, an antiquarian, scholar, and coroner by profession. S.R.M.D. or S. Rhiogail Ma Dhream was the motto of S.L. MacGregor Mathers, the translator of *The Greater Key of King Solomon*, the *Book of the Sacred Magic of Abramelin the Mage*, and *The Qabalah Unveiled*, which latter consisted of certain portions of the Zohar prefixed by an introduction of high erudition. He also employed the Latin motto Deo Duce Comite Ferro, S.D.A. was the abbreviation of the motto Sapiens Dominabitur Astris chosen by a Fräulein Anna Sprengel of Nüremberg, Germany. Such were the actors on this occult stage, this the *dramatis personae* in the background of the commencement of the Order. More than any other figures who may later have prominently figured in its government and work, these are the four outstanding figures publicly involved in the English foundation of what came to be known as The Hermetic Order of the Golden Dawn.

How the actual beginning came to pass is not really known. Or rather, because of so many conflicting stories and legends the truth is impossible to discover. At any rate, so far as England is concerned, without a doubt we must seek for its origins in the Societas Rosicruciana in Anglia. This was an organisation formulated in 1865 by eminent Freemasons, some of them claiming Rosicrucian initiation from continental authorities. Amongst those who claimed such initiation was one Kenneth Mackenzie, a Masonic scholar and encyclopaedist, who had received his at the hands of a Count Apponyi in Austria. The objects of this Society, which confined its membership to Freemasons in good standing, was "to afford mutual aid and encouragement in working out the great problems of Life, and in discovering the secrets of nature; to facilitate the study of the systems of philosophy founded upon the Kaballah and the doctrines of Hermes Trismegistus." Dr. Westcott also remarks that to-day its Fratres "are concerned in the study and administration of medicines, and in their manufacture upon old lines; they also teach and practise the curative effects of coloured light, and cultivate mental processes which are believed to induce spiritual enlightenment and extended powers of the human senses, especially in the directions of clairvoyance and clairaudience."

The first Chief of this Society, its Supreme Magus so-called, was one Robert Wentworth Little, who is said to have rescued some old rituals from a certain Masonic storeroom, and it was from certain of those papers that the Society's rituals were elaborated. He died in 1878 and in his stead was appointed Dr. William R. Woodman. Both Dr. Westcott and MacGregor Mathers were prominent and active members of this body. If fact, the former became Supreme Magus upon Woodman's death, the office of junior Magus being conferred upon Mathers. One legend has it that one day Westcott discovered in his library a series of cipher manuscripts, and in order to decipher them he enlisted the aid of MacGregor Mathers. It is said that this library was that of the Societas Rosicruciana in Anglia, and it is likewise asserted that those cipher manuscripts, were among the rituals and documents originally rescued by Robert Little from Freemason's Hall. Yet other accounts have it that Westcott found the manuscripts on a bookstall in Farringdon Street. Further apocryphal legends claim that they were found in the library of books and manuscripts inherited from the mystic and clairvoyant, Frederick Hockley who died in 1885. Whatever the real origin of these mysterious cipher manuscripts, when eventually deciphered with the aid of MacGregor Mathers, they were alleged to have contained the address of Fräulein Anna Sprengel who proported to be a Rosicrucian Adept, in Nüremberg. Here was a discovery which, naturally, not for one moment was neglected. Its direct result was a lengthy correspondence with Fräulin Sprengel, culminating in the transmission of authority to Woodman, Westcott and Mathers, to formulate in England a semi-public occult organisations which was to employ an elaborate magical ceremonial, Qabalistic teaching, and a comprehensive scheme of spiritual training. Its foundation was designed to include both men and women on a basis of perfect equality in contradistinction to the policy of the Societas Rosicruciana in Anglia which was comprised wholly of Freemasons. Thus, in 1887, the Hermetic Order of the Golden Dawn was established. Its first English Temple, Isis-Urania, was opened in the following year.

There is a somewhat different version as to its origin, having behind it the authority of Frater F.R. the late Dr. Felkin, who was the Chief of the Stella Matutina as well as a member of the Societas Rosicruciana. According to his account, and the following words are substantially his own, prior to 1880 members of the Rosicrucian Order on the Continent selected with great care their own candidates whom they thought suitable for personal instruction. For these pupils they were each individually responsible, the pupils thus selected being trained by them in the theoretical traditional knowledge now used in the Outer Order. After some three or four more years of intensive private study they were presented to the Chiefs of the Order, and if approved and passed by examination, they then received their initiation into the Order of the Roseae Rubeae et Aureae Crucis.

The political state of Europe in those days was such that the strictest secrecy as to the activities of these people was very necessary. England, however, where many Masonic bodies and semi-private organisations were flourishing without interference, was recognised as having far greater freedom and liberty than the countries in which the continental Adepts were domiciled. Some, but by no means all, suggested therefore that in England open Temple work might be inaugurated. And Dr. Felkin here adds, though without the least word of explanation as to what machinery was set in motion towards the attainment of that end, "and so it was... It came about then that Temples arose in London, Bradford, Weston-super-Mare, and Edinburgh. The ceremonies we have were elaborated from manuscripts, and all went well for a time."

As to what ensued after that inauguration of Temple work here we have little record, though an unorthodox account written by Aleister Crowley continues this historical theme in substantially the same words as were orally communicated to me by the late Imperator of one of the now-existent Temples. "After some time S.D.A. died; further requests for help were met with a prompt refusal from the colleagues of S.D.A. It was written by one of them that S.D.A.'s schemes had always been regarded with disapproval but since the absolute rule of the Adepts is never to interfere with the judgment of any other person whomsoever—how much more, than one of themselves, and that one most highly revered!—they had refrained from active opposition. The Adept who wrote this added that the Order had already quite enough knowledge to enable it or its members to formulate a magical link with the adepts. Shortly after this, one called S.R.M.D. announced that he had formulated such a link, and that himself with two others was to govern the Order... We content ourselves, then, with observing that the death of one of his two colleagues, and the weakness of the other, secured to S.R.M.D., the sole authority..."

In elaboration of this statement, it may be said that in 1891 Dr. Woodman died after but a few days illness, leaving the management of the Order to Westcott and Mathers. Evidently these two scholars carried on quite well together for about six years, for the indications are that the Order flourished and grew expansive. Exactly why Westcott withdrew from the Order—for this is the next major occurrence—appears difficult to discover. Concerning this also several versions are extant. One account has it that accidently he left some of the Order manuscripts in a portfolio bearing a signature in a cab, and the driver upon finding them turned them over to the authorities. Since Westcott was by profession an East London coroner, the medical authorities strongly objected that one in an official capacity should, no matter how remotely, be connected with anything that savoured occult. It was suggested to him therefore that he must withdraw from the Order or else resign his post as coroner, since the two were considered in those days incompatibles. He chose to resign his post as coroner, since the two were considered in those days incompatibles. He chose to resign from the Order. Yet again it is suggested that it was simply a personal quarrel that led to the parting of the ways with Mathers, which does seem the more probable explanation. Whatever the cause, some six years after the death of Dr. Woodman, Westcott withdrew from the Order, which was thus left to the sole authority of Mathers.

The pamphlet on Rosicrucian history then proceeds in narrative that following Westcott's resignation from "this association in 1897, the English Temples soon after fell into abeyance." This reads like an instance of wish-fulfillment. Though fairly near the essential truth of the matter, it is not quite in accordance with fact. Following the resignation of Westcott, Mathers resigned within his Order as supreme autocrat. Judging from the evidence at our disposal he was not a particularly benevolent one, for many were the misunderstandings that ruffled the mystic placidity of his Temples, and several of the individuals who dared so much as differ or argue with him were promptly expelled, and flung into the outer darkness. Presumably spiritual pride was the flaw in his armour, and he seemed to harbour quite a few delusions. One of the latter was his conveyance to the body of Adepti as a piece of objective everyday experience, that whilst in the Bois de Boulogne one day he was approached by three Adepts who confirmed him in the sole rulership of the Order. On the strength of his supposed occurrence, he issued to the Theorici of the grade of Adeptus Minor as powerfully worded manifesto, naming himself in no uncertain terms as a chosen vessel and demanding from all those who received the manifesto a signed oath of personal loyalty and allegiance. Those who refused to send a written statement of voluntary submission to him were either expelled from the Order or degraded to a lower rank.

Meanwhile, a considerable amount of discontent had been slowly brewing amongst the Order members. Dissatisfaction with the autocratic leadership of S.R.M.D. was growing very steadily and persistently. No definite or clear-cut reasons appear to be given for this, for evidently this restlessness had been gradually fructifying whilst the hypertrophy of Mathers' ego was becoming more and more pronounced. Some say that S.R.M.D. was guilty of innumerable magical tricks of a particularly irresponsible nature which eventually brought disrepute both upon himself and the Order of which he was head. Others, more romantically minded, claimed that his English translation of *The Sacred Magic of Abramelin the Mage* was a powerful magical act which attracted to his sphere forces of evil so terrible in nature that he was wholly unable to withstand them. Frater F.R. propounds the more rational view that it was simply spiritual pride and love of power which so gained the ascendancy that he demanded of the members of his organisation a personal fealty and obedience to his own personality instead of the work itself. How very familiar all this sounds. In one form or another, it is the story of the same unhappy fate which dogs and finally ruins every religious and spiritual community. By changing these names, Theosophists may recognise a very homely story.[2]

In claiming his right to unquestioned leadership, and when refusing to appoint two others of the body of Adepti to fill the vacant posts of co-Chiefs, Mathers also promised some of the more advanced members of the Second Order additional grades in the path of Adeptship and even more esoteric teaching. These, apparently, were not forthcoming—though it must be confessed that regardless of the personal shortcomings of Mathers as a leader or as a writer, it is patent that there was a vast knowledge and a deep and wide erudition concealed with him. Naturally the Adepti gave utterance to their complete disapproval of this delay in the fulfilment of their Chief's promises, gradually coming to insist that he had neither the knowledge nor the grades to impart. Further unpleasant bickering drew forth from Mathers the retort that he was certainly not going to waste either his grades or knowledge on such hopeless duffers as they were. And in any event, he was Chief and leader; their further progress, if there was to be any, must be left entirely in his hands. In short, a virulent quarrel was in process of development, and though for quite a long time it fermented beneath the surface, it finally culminated in a group of the Adepti forming a strong combination to expel their chief S.R.M.D. just prior to the actual appearance of the schism, and whilst yet the

---

[2] As may knowledgeable, modern-day students of the Golden Dawn.

rebellion was gaining impetus, certain events happened which call here not for elucidation, since that is impossible, but simply for registration.

About this time, a certain Mrs. Rose Horos approached Mathers who came to acknowledge her as an initiate of a high grade. Exactly why, it is again impossible to say definitely. It was stated in defence of Mathers that Mrs. Horos was able to repeat to him a certain conversation he had had years previously when he visited Madame Blavatsky at Denmark Hill, and the repetition of this scrap of conversation convinced him of her status. Anyway, it was a sad piece of deception, and an unhappy acknowledgement on the part of Mathers indicating his complete lack of judgment and insight into character. Mrs. Horos and her husband were very soon discovered to be sex-perverts of the worst description. Nor was this all, for it is alleged that they were also responsible for the theft from Mathers of a complete set of Order documents. It seems incredible that Mathers could have been so gullible, for that is the only word which adequately describes his stupidity, as to accept without further verification the occult claim of his woman, giving her access to the rituals and teaching of the Golden Dawn. Subsequently the immoral activities of these two people having attracted the attention of the police, they were arrested. In December 1901 at their trial, the Order of the Golden Dawn was given unpleasant and unjustified publicity by being associated with the chequered careers of these two persons. In the witness box the male prisoner made the remark concerning the Golden Dawn Neophyte obligation that it "was prepared by the Chiefs of the Order who are in India"—which of course was a farrago of nonsense, but unfortunately just the type of nonsense which survives for many years. He was sentenced to fifteen years penal servitude, and his wife to seven. Around this period also, one Florence Farr, whose esoteric motto was Soror S.S.D.D., having for some years been left in charge of Isis-Urania Temple while Mathers continued his research work in Paris, decided for various personal reasons to enter her resignation from that important post. Under date of February 16th 1900, Mathers, writing from Paris, refused to accept her resignation, believing that she intended to "form a combination to make a schism therein with the idea of working secretly or avowedly under Sapere Aude." In this same letter, he was responsible for the astonishing statement that S.A. had never been at any time in touch with Fräulin Sprengel of Nüremberg but had "either himself forged or procured to be forged the professional correspondence between him and her." As was only to be expected this letter came as a overwhelming surprise to S.S.D.D., who was thoroughly stunned by this accusation of dishonesty and forgery levelled against S.A. After contemplating the whole situation in an almost frantic state of mind for several days in the country, she finally communicated with S.A asking him to corroborate or deny the accusations. Her next act was to form a Committee of Seven within the Second Order to investigate the allegations made. This Committee asked S.R.M.D. to produce for his own sake and for the sake of the Order proof of the accuracy of his statements. Because, they argued, since it was upon the authority of this alleged correspondence that the Order was founded, the historical position of the Order as descended from Mediaeval Rosicrucian sources collapsed should it be proven that the correspondence had been forged. This viewpoint was not altogether accurate, for while S.R.M.D. had stated that S.A.

had never been in touch with S.D.A., he never denied that he himself had not been in constant communication with her. Then followed a lengthy correspondence which afterwards was collected and printed in the form of a long dossier. In fine, Mathers refused unconditionally to acknowledge the authority or even the existence of the Committee nor would he produce proof of any kind to substantiate his claim that S.A. had forged Second Order communications. It goes without saying of course that S.A. fervently denied the truth of these allegation of forgery, but all the same he refused to do anything about it.

No good purpose could possibly be served by enlarging upon the unhappy events which immediately followed. To a large extent the history of the Order is so confused and muddled at this juncture, and the rumours which have come down to us so chaotic and contradictory, that it has proved wholly impossible to extricate the truth from the foul débris of slander, abuse and recrimination. A clear picture of what occurred seems impossible to recover. It would appear, to state the matter simply, that Mathers expelled the rebels who then formed a schism. On the other hand, it is also held that he was himself expelled by the revolting wing from his own Order and left with about half a dozen adherents, with whose assistance, moral and financial, he continued his Temple.

As their first magical gesture of independence, the rebels changed the name of the Order to The Stella Matutina. Ruled for a year by a committee of twelve, developments forced them to realise that this was far from a satisfactory arrangement. Inasmuch, however, as it had taken several years first to brew and then to develop into an open gesture of defiance, the spirit which conceived the rebellion was not thus at a single stroke to be banished. Having elevated the standard of revolt by expelling their former chief, for many a dismal month was the Stella Matutina haunted by that ghost. After almost inconceivable pettiness and dispute, the rebels were at the end persuaded by circumstance to abandon every feature of their reform to return to the original scheme of appointing Three Chiefs to govern and lead them. Even this, later, was abandoned if not officially then in practice, for a virtual autocracy similar to that enjoyed by Mathers was once again instituted, though on a much smaller scale. The revolt had been in vain. Those finally selected and appointed as the Chiefs were Fratres Sub Spe, Finem Respice, and Sacramentum Regis. These three Fratres conducted the Order of the Stella Matutina in harmony for about a year. Then, for various reasons, Sacramentum Regis chose to resign. At the meetings held to appoint his successor, differences of the most trivial character continued to arise. Indeed, the spirit of fraternity and wisdom had departed, leaving its averse antithesis, the venom of destruction, to dwell in their midst. Another split developed. Apparently one wind of the schism, thoroughly alarmed in all its bourgeous incompetence and fear by the recent disturbances to the peace of the Order, attributed that cycle of catastrophe to the occult content of the Order teaching, and because of this were now desirous of casting aside as valueless, from the spiritual point of view, the whole of the magical tradition. Their intention was to retain a sort of indeterminate Mysticism of the type which has so often brought disrepute upon the subject, coming to regard their Temple as an adjunct, a clandestine back-door to the Church in some one of its many forms—with especial attractions, I believe, to the Anglo-Catholic groups. One other and more important group within the schism, led by Fratres Finem Respice and Sub Spe carried on full Temple work, more or less adhering to the original plan of the Golden Dawn routine as laid down in the documents drawn up by MacGregor Mathers.

Thus we find in place of a consolidated fraternity at least three separate groupings of individuals engaged in the practice of the Golden Dawn ceremonial system in open Temple, perpetuating as best they might the traditions of the Magic of Light. There was, first, the diminutive group under the leadership of S.R.M.D., still retaining the original Order name. To him were still loyal the Temple or Temples that a few years prior to the final crash had been instituted in the United States of America. Both F.R. and S.S. were in charge of a Stella Matutina Temple, and it is my belief that after a while even they parted company and conducted separate groups, the one in London calling itself the Amoun Temple, and the latter in Edinburgh, Amen-Ra by name. In London also, a separate Temple was being conducted by Frater Sacramentum Regis calling itself the Reconstructed Rosicrucian Order, a group characterised by its exclusive devotion to Christian Mysticism, its rituals being elaborated into verbose and interminable parades of turgidity.

Formerly united by a single fraternal bond, we now see several Temples being conducted by different groupings of individuals who, while pretending to fraternal communion, had but little sympathy with and affection for the sister Temples of the schism. The slander that was invented and swiftly circulated, as only malice can be circulated, is unrepeatable. Few individuals of real worth were exempt from this network of scandal which enmeshed the whole organisation. This man was an adulterer, a dipsomaniac—and even after the lapse of more than thirty years this slander is still current. So thoroughly had the central unity of the Order broken up that each of these Stella Matutina Temples appointed its own Imperator, Cancellarius and Praemonstrator, considering itself by these gestures an autonomous occult body. Thus began the downfall of organised magical instruction through the semi-esoteric channels of the Hermetic Order of the Golden Dawn. Whatever else should be insisted upon in Magic, unity is the prime essential. A united body of manifestation at all costs should have been maintained. And the old adage "United we stand, divided we fall" is no idle phrase, especially since the elimination of the "heresy of separateness" is one of the cardinal injunctions of the Great Work. The separate Temples decided to fall independently of how or why or where the other groups fell. Each was smug, complacent and fully confident that it alone continued the magical tradition. The result is that to-day those original Temples are either dead or moribund. While they may have given rise to yet other groups, there is not one of the latter which is not in a diseased condition.

One can hardly help recalling the bitter admonition given by S.R.M.D. to the organisers of the schism. He said, in effect, and in the later years Frater Sub Spe corroborated that statement, that he was the principal Chief of the Order by whom and through whom the Order had originally been organised to disseminate the magical tradition. Remember, he warned, what happened to the Theosophical Society after Blavatsky had departed, and there began the disintegration of the world-wide society she had founded and fed with her own life blood. Certainly Mathers' prophecy seems to have vindicated itself. Just as there are innumerable sects claiming to be the original Theosophical Society and professing allegiance to the principles taught by Blavatsky, so are there now several decaying Temples claiming unbroken descent from the original Isis-Urania. Each insists fervently that it alone is the genuine Order; all others are schismatic and unimportant. To-day, as stated above, not one of these surviving Temples is in an even moderately healthy condition. Nor have they ever been since the early days of their foundation. An amusing sidelight on human nature is disclosed by the fact that in one of the Obligations retained by the schismatic groups, there is still the original clause, "Do you further undertake not to be a stirrer up of strife, of schism, or of opposition to the chiefs."

It was towards the close of 1989, just prior to the revolt, that Aleister Crowley was introduced to the Order by Frater Volo Noscere, receiving his Neophyte initiation at Mark Mason's Hall. It was clear, soon after he joined, that here was a highly gifted young man, and that in many ways, though unrestrained and undisciplined, his was a powerfully magical personality. From Captain J.F.C. Fuller's rather verbose and flamboyant account in the Equinox we gather that Crowley was advanced through the grades of the Order quickly, and assimilated the routine knowledge without the least difficulty. Those grades which were not formally separated by automatic delays, were taken at the rate of one a month, and the succeeding ones at the prescribed intervals of three, seven and nine months. By the time he had taken his Portal grade, the revolt was in full swing, the wisdom and authority of the Chief being on every side doubted and challenged. It was around this period, too, that Crowley's morals and alleged pernicious conduct offended those who were conducting Temple work in London, and the ruling Adepti of Isis-Urania refused to advance him further They refused to do this in spite of the deliberate warning contained in Mathers' manifesto previously mentioned: "What I discountenance and will check and punish whenever I find it in the Order is the attempt to criticise and interfere with the private life of members of the Order... The private life of a person is a matter between himself or herself and his or her God." Whether Mathers was impressed by the promise of Crowley's personality, or whether he decided upon his next step to show contempt for the ruling Chiefs of Isis-Urania Temple, we do not know. But, soon after, Crowley was invited to Paris where he received the grade of Adeptus Minor from Mathers in Ahathoor Temple. This act served but to inflame the differences which were now openly separating Mathers from his erstwhile followers, and increased the bitter hatred which the Order members bore and still bear for Crowley.

To Crowley's credit, it must be conceded that when open revolt did flame forth, at least he sided with S.R.M.D., acting as his plenipotentiary in the proposed meetings with the rebels in London. The Adepti, however, unconditionally refused to recognise or have ought to do with Crowley. In his fantastic gard of a Highland chieftain with kilt, dirks and tartan, and his face concealed by a heavy mask, he did assuredly make himself so great a laughing stock on that occasion as to make it difficult for anyone to take him seriously.

The conjunction of two headstrong and egotistical personalities rendered it most probable that sooner or later Crowley and Mathers should quarrel. They did, and each went his separate way. Many and varied again are the fantastic accounts of the reasons for that separation. But no matter what their cause, some three years afterwards events led Crowley to denounce Mathers as one obsessed either by Abramelin demons or by the evil personalities of the then incarcerated Horos couple, and that he himself had been nominated by the Secret Chiefs of the Invisible Order to be the outer head of the visible organisation. In the various numbers of the *Equinox*, the official organ of Crowley's personal reformulation of the Order system under the title A∴A—which does not signify "Atlantean Adepts" as supposed by some stupid review in the Occult Review—may be found Crowley's more or less garbled version of the Order teaching and ceremonial.

At this juncture, it is needful to contradict denials on the part of certain Order members that Crowley did not obtain full Order teaching. Some of these denials are entirely too vehement and "methinks the lady doth protest too much." First of all, I am fully convinced from a close and prolonged study of all Crowley's literary output that he did obtain his Adeptus Minor grade from Mathers after the London group refused to advance him. Unquestionably this is true. Nevertheless, even if this were not the case, he was the *intime*, so to say, of Fratres Volo Noscere and Yehi Aour, both advanced members of the grade of Adeptus Minor, who coached and trained him so that he benefitted by their knowledge and wide experience. Whatever knowledge these Fratres had received from the Order documents was given to Crowley. There is little, I imagine, that he did not receive of the Order documents was given to Crowley. There is little, I imagine, that he did not receive of the Order teaching then extant, whatever may have been the means fair or foul by which he obtained that teaching. And while he did not publish it in its entirety, it is possible to perceive from hints scattered here, there, and everywhere, that very little had been kept from him. Any student who has a bird's-eye view of the Order system will recognise traces of every aspect of it in the different volumes of Crowley's literary fecundity.

Had Crowley published the entire body of knowledge, only slightly editing the redundancy and verbose complexity of Mather's literary style—had he issued that teaching so that it bore some semblance to its original state to indicate what it really was and how practised within the Temple—his exposé might not have been too serious. It is possible that he might have been acknowledged as a benefactor of mankind, even if later on he did ruin his own personal reputation by broadcasting absurd legends and leading a foolishly dissipated life. But it was his special mode of publication which argued against the advisability of partially disclosing the secret knowledge of the Order. He tampered unnecessarily with the Grade rituals, so that their beauty as well as practical worth was gone.[3] It became impossible to form any estimation of the efficacy or construction of those ceremonies from their mutilated shadows in the *Equinox*. Perhaps his aim was to eliminate important parts of the rites and practical work so that interested people, realising that more information was required, would communicate with him for further guidance, thus enabling him to consolidate his position as a leader, and

---

[3] It is statements like these that have led Crowley-deifiers to hate and ignore Regardie. Anyone who gives Crowley a fair read will find that much of what he wrote is pure crap. All too often his followers have elevated the garbage to gospel while ignoring the good stuff. Such is the process of Biblification. In the world of organized religion, truth must be eliminated as a threat to self-aggrandizing dogma. [Ed.]

formulate an active Order. This is certainly true of the instruction, for example, on Geomancy. The rituals and teaching were badly mauled, rearranged out of all recognition to their former state, and then surrounded by Yoga instructions, short stories, articles on sex-Magic, poetry—much of it of a dubious nature—and a host of miscellaneous odds and ends.

With Crowley's instruction in the art of Yoga, printed both within and without the *Equinox*, there can be no quarrel. They are amongst the clearest ever produced on the subject and amongst the finest examples of the excellent prose of which Crowley was capable. We, the occult-reading public, are immeasurably the richer for their appearance. Epigrams, short stories, card-games, and libels on former friends, however, can hardly be considered fit companions for occult teaching. It is my confirmed belief that it is practically impossible, without more precise guidance or tuition, to ascertain from the *Equinox* and Crowley's other literary productions exactly what is the actual nature of Magic as a definite practical scheme. His form of presentation, and the other contents of the *Equinox*, creating nothing but confusion.

Though a revelation of the inner teaching of the Golden Dawn would have been a boon to mankind, yet manifestly Crowley's manner of presentation ruined the effort. If the breaking of a sacred obligation is at all justifiable—as occasionally it is—it is so only when the matter covered by that oath is revealed in a dignified manner and with a noble spirit, as well as in a style fitting to its intrinsic nature. In such an event, the oath is neither betrayed nor profaned, for in being abrogated on behalf of mankind, the author becomes duly qualified to speak for those with whom alone is the power to bind or loose.

It is not my wish to retract what nearly three years ago I enthusiastically wrote in *The Tree of Life*. It was then my conviction as it is now that there was much of a highly important nature in what this extraordinary man of genius has written and published. But I am also profoundly impressed by this fact. Unless one has first studied Magic from a more comprehensible and reliable source, most of what he has written, albeit based upon his own practical experience, will be in the main unintelligible. Any student who has gained a sympathetic understanding of the Golden Dawn teaching will be capable of discriminating between the futile reprehensible portions of Crowley's work, and of deciding which part of it is worth-while addition to an already magnificent system. And it is because Crowley concedes to his own credit in his, in many respects, admirable volume entitled *Magick* that he has done Magic inestimable service by reason of his development of it, that I have considered it imperative, together with a number of other reasons of equal urgency, to place the Golden Dawn system before the public. Crowley's claims are, in my estimation, wholly exaggerated. I am far from being convinced that the scheme of theory and practice presented in his literature—extraordinary though it is in many ways, considering that it is a development of the simple basic Golden Dawn material—is equal in any way to the system put into documentary form by S.L. MacGregor Mathers and his colleagues.

PREFACES
by Israel Regardie

GEMS FROM THE EQUINOX

ALL THE MAGICAL WRITINGS

Instructions by Aleister Crowley
for His own Magical Order

Edited by Israel Regardie

GEMS FROM THE EQUINOX
All The Magical Writings
Instructions by Aleister Crowley
for His own Magical Order
Preface by Israel Regardie
Llewellyn Publications, First Printing, 1974

Between 1909 and 1914, Aleister Crowley published in England a large, beautifully printed periodical entitled *The Equinox*. The masthead on the cover bore two phrases, "The Aim of Religion" and "The Method of Science." It contained a wide assortment of verse, plays, short stories and miscellaneous occult material. One issue appeared every six months at the Spring and Autumnal Equinoxes of that five-year period. Ten enormous issues appeared in all. One thousand and fifty copies were produced at each equinoctial printing, fifty copies being bound in white buckram for the subscription trade, the rest being bound in boards.

After 1914 there was a hiatus of five years, corresponding to World War I, when Crowley was domiciled in the United States. He called it a five-year period of silence. Following this, one large volume, bound in blue cloth, made its solitary appearance. It has been called colloquially *The Blue Equinox*. And that was it. None were published thereafter. There was no more money available: there were no more *Equinoxes*.

Originally they were published to sell for about five shillings, then for half a guinea each–in those halcyon days about two dollars and fifty cents per volume. They did not sell very well. Had sales been better, enough revenue might have been forthcoming to have permitted the continuation of the publishing project for a longer period of time.

Nevertheless, within a few years, the ten issues of volume I were commanding a premium of one hundred dollar per set– had any been available. Today I am told that the going price is five hundred dollars or more per set! But to obtain a set is practically impossible.

By students of occultism, these volumes were regarded as a veritable gold mine of occult lore. Most who bought them were far less interested in the wide literary assortment offered. Yoga and Magick were what these books stood for, and this is where they excelled.

There was simply nothing like them elsewhere. In these instructions about the occult arts, Crowley had used superb prose, and had clarified the subject matter by eliminating all the superstition, dross and fantasy that had been attached to these topics. They were masterpieces of instruction. It was for these reasons that the several volumes of *The Equinox* were so zealously sought after throughout the years.

Crowley himself felt that it was the first serious attempt to publicize the facts about the occult arts since Madame Blavatsky wrote *Isis Unveiled*, though there is very little connection between the latter and *The Equinox*, as Blavatsky never recommended the occult arts for the average human being. Crowley felt his was the first venture to forward the method of science and the aim of religion with scholarship and commonsense. He was inordinately proud of having inaugurated an epoch in publishing. It imposed a standard of "sincerity, scholarship, scientific seriousness and aristocracy of all kinds, from the excellence of its English to the perfection of its printing" on all those interested in this topic.

Though he recognized the small public it appealed to his enthusiasts informed him that it was regarded as the standard publication of its kind which had been quoted, copied and imitated everywhere. It has been said that some occult societies have been founded by charlatans on no other authority than its subject matter. Its influence has changed the whole current of thought of students of this subject all over the world.

In one of the letters comprising *Magick without Tears* (published in 1973 by Lleywellyn Publications), Crowley has written a few words concerning his original intent regarding *The Equinox*. What he had to say is so interesting that the following is quoted from that letter:

> My special job was to preserve the Sacred Tradition, so that a new Renaissance might in due season rekindle the hidden Light. I was accordingly to make a Quintessence of the Ancient Wisdom, and publish it in as permanent a form as possible. This I did in *The Equinox*. I should perhaps have been strictly classical, and admitted only the "Publication in Class A," "A-B," "B," and "D" material. But I had the idea that it would be a good plan to add all sorts of other stuff, so that people who were not in any way interested in real Work might preserve their copies... "They" [the Secret Chiefs of the Order]...were agreed on measures calculated to assure the survival of the Wisdom worth saying until the time, perhaps in three hundred or six hundred years later, when a new current should revive the shattered thought of mankind. *The Equinox*, in a word, was to be a sort of Rosetta Stone.

It seems as though he recognized that he should really have published only the Official Instructions of the Order in order to preserve the "Sacred Tradition." Now that the original sets of *The Equinox* are no longer available, it seems necessary to reissue the fundamental material that he had in mind at the start–the official instructions. If it was the wish of the so-called Secret Chiefs of the Order to preserve the practical wisdom of the hidden sanctuaries against the disasters of war, natural cataclysm, and partisan censorship–all of which seem clearly once more in the offing–I hope that this volume, *Gems from The Equinox*, will assist in the fulfillment of his original magical intention, freed from the addition of "all sorts of other stuff." The essentials of the sacred tradition can stand by themselves without dilution of any kind whatsoever.

Periodically, criticisms of *The Equinox* reach me that are not too dissimilar to those at one time levelled at *The Golden Dawn* (St. Paul: Llewellyn Publications, 1970). Some students have felt this enormous mass of instruction to be overwhelming and just too much for them. The result was that they go confused, and could do nothing with what otherwise they recognized to be invaluable.

However, I feel the classification of this material in the manner depicted here may simplify things so as to enable the student to grasp it and find his way through the maze more readily. He will then come to understand the basic theme that Crowley laid down in his Order. It can best be described by quoting Crowley verbatim from an editorial that appeared in one of the volumes of *The Equinox*.

> I have been asked by Authority to say a few words on the relations which should subsist between a Neophyte and his Probationers. Though a Neophyte is obliged to show "zeal in service" towards his probationers, it is no part of his duty to be continually beating the tattoo. He has his own work to do–very serious and important work–and he cannot be expected to spend all his time in making silk purses out of pigs' ears. He is not expected to set definite tasks, nor has he authority to do so. The Probationer is purposely left to himself, as the object of

probation is principally that those in authority may discover the nature of the raw material. It is the duty of the Probationer to perform the exercises recommended in his text-books, and to submit the record of his results for criticism. If he finds himself in a difficulty, or if any unforeseen result occurs, he should communicate with his Neophyte, and he should remember that although he is permitted to select the practices which appeal to him, he is expected to show considerable acquaintance with all of them. More than acquaintance, it should be experience; otherwise what is he to do when as a Neophyte he is consulted by his Probationers? It is important that he should be armed at all points, and I am authorised to say that no one will be admitted as a Neophyte unless his year's work gives evidence of considerable attainment in the fundamental practices: Asana, Pranayama, assumption of God-forms, vibration of divine names, rituals of banishing and invoking, and the practices set out in sections 5 and 6 of *Liber O*. Although he is not examined in any of these, the elementary experience is necessary in order that he may intelligently assist those who will be under him.

But let no one imagine that those in authority will urge probationers to work hard. Those who are incapable of hard work may indeed be pushed along, but the moment that the pressure is removed they will fall back, and it is not the purpose of the A∴A∴ to do anything else than to make its students independent and free. Full instructions have been placed within the reach of everybody; let them see to it that they make full use of that instruction.

The newcomer to this occult field might begin to wonder what all this fuss was about. What were these exercises or experiments for? What did they accomplish? What was the so-called Great Work?

Again, these questions can most readily be answered by quoting directly from Crowley. His own words from *The Equinox* provide an eloquent answer to these and similar questions. The following set of statements shows what Crowley thought, and how excellently he expressed those thoughts.

MISTAKES OF MYSTICS

I. Since truth is supra-rational, it is incommunicable in the language of reason.
II. Hence all mystics have written nonsense, and what sense they have written is so far untrue.
III. Yet as a still lake yields a truer reflection of the sun than a torrent, he whose mind is best balanced will, if he become a mystic, become the best mystic.

THE METHOD OF EQUILIBRIUM

I. THE PASSIONS, Etc.

I. Since the ultimate truth of teleology is unknown, all codes of morality are arbitrary.
II. Therefore the student has no concern with ethics as such.
III. He is consequently free "to do his duty in that state of life to which it has pleased God to call him."

II. THE REASON

I. Since truth is supra-rational, any rational statement is false.
II. Let the student then contradict every proposition that presents itself to him.
III. Rational ideas being thus expelled from the mind, there is room for the apprehension of spiritual truth. It should be remarked that this does not destroy the validity of reasonings on their own plane.

III. THE SPIRITUAL SENSORIUM

I. Man being a finite being, he is incapable of apprehending the infinite. Nor does his communion with infinite being (true or false) alter this fact.
II. Let then the student contradict every vision and refuse to enjoy it; first, because there is certainly another vision possible of precisely contradictory nature; secondly, because though he is God, he is also a man upon an insignificant planet. Being thus equilibrated laterally and vertically, it may be that, either by affirmation or denial of all these things together, he may attain the supreme trance.

IV. THE RESULT

I. Trance is defined as the ek-stasis of one particular tract of the brain, caused by meditating on the idea corresponding to it.
II. Let the student therefore beware lest in that idea be any trace of imperfection. It should be pure, balanced, calm, complete, fitted in every way to dominate the mind, as it will. Even as in the choice of a king to be crowned.
III. So will the decrees of this king be just and wise as he was just and wise before he was made king. The life and work of the mystic will reflect (though dimly) the supreme guiding force of the mystic, the highest trance to which he has attained.

YOGA AND MAGIC

I. Yoga is the art of uniting the mind to a single idea. It has four methods.

    Gnana-Yoga   Union by Knowledge
    Raja-Yoga   Union by Will
    Bhakta-Yoga   Union by Love
    Hatha-Yoga   Union by Courage
    add Mantra-Yoga Union through Speech
    Karma-Yoga   Union through Work

These are united by the supreme method of Silence.

II. Ceremonial Magic is the art of uniting the mind to a single idea. It has four Methods:

    The Holy Qabalah   Union by Knowledge
    The Sacred Magic   Union by Will
    The Acts of Worship Union of Love
    The Ordeals   Union of Courage
    add The Invocations Union through Speech
    The Acts of Service Union through Work

These are united by the supreme method of Silence.

III. If this idea be any but the Supreme and Perfect idea, and the student lose control, the result is insanity, obsession, fanaticism, or paralysis and death (add addiction to gossip and incurable idleness) according to the nature of the failure. Let then the Student understand all these things and combine them in his Art, uniting them by supreme methods of Silence.

One of the prime motives for the publication of *The Equinox* was to provide an avenue of expression for Crowley's own magical Order named the A∴A∴. In addition, he wanted a medium through which he could voice his attitudes toward the Hermetic Order of the Golden Dawn to which he had once belonged.

It was really unfortunate that this entry into that Order, practical work in Magick and meditation prescribed for the first several grades of the A∴A∴.

A Syllabus of the Official Instructions of A∴A∴, extrapolated from *The Equinox*, vol. I, no. 10. There is a later, more complete syllabus in *The Blue Equinox*, but it contains a large number of items which have never been published. I am including a few pages from the latter because it does provide a list of books for general reading which I can endorse.

Section II. The Book of the Law

Liber AL vel Legis. This is the reproduction of the text as given in *The Equinox*, vol. I, no. 10. The basis of the whole work as laid down by Crowley, it is the document dictated to him in Cairo in 1904. The history of this unique experience is given at length in *The Temple of Solomon the King* and in his newly published biography. I have also discussed some aspects of it from a different point of view in *The Eye in the Triangle*.

Liber CCC: Khabs Am Pekht; Liber CL: De Lege Libellvm. Both of these papers are elementary commentaries on *The Book of the Law*. There is in existence an elaborate extenuation of *Liber Legis* far more elaborate than these two documents, which has not yet seen the light of publication. It is an extremely important commentary in the sense that it elaborates what Crowley came to think and believe and feel about this book.

Liber Nv. This represents a series of meditations predicted on *Liber AL vel Legis*.

Liber Had. This is also a series of meditations predicated on *Liber AL vel Legis,* in order to derive practical experience of what that book speaks of.

Section III. Yoga

Liber E. vel Exercitiorvm. This document provides basic training in a number of root disciples. In one sense it is that piece of instruction without which more advanced training can have little meaning. It is written clearly, simply and in a straightforward manner.

Liber Rv. Clear and unmuddled instruction in pranayama, the breathing exercises that comprise so large a part of Yoga.

These last two papers should be studied in conjunction with two other works of Crowley's: Part I of *Book 4* and *Eight Lectures on Yoga* (Dallas: Sangreal Foundation, 1969).

Liber Astarte. A simply written but beautiful instruction on Bhakta Yoga, the yoga of devotion. It demonstrates Crowley at his best; it is a splendid piece of writing.

Liber III vel Jvgorvm. An uncomplicated technique for the development of Will and for establishing conditioned responses to be used in the control of the mind. At first reading, it may sound repulsive to some "sweet and lighters," but from personal experimentation with it years ago I can strongly recommend it. It is highly efficacious.

Liber HHH. This is a presentation of some Tantra disciplines. One section is the outcome of work with a Golden Dawn document analyzing the Neophyte Ritual, as described at some length in *The Eye in the Triangle.* The second part is a meditation predicated on what the Buddhists call the ten impurities. The final one is a method of raising the Kundalini.

Liber Tvrris. A discipline for achieving what Patanjali has described as "hindering the modifications of the thinking principle." Its accomplishment demands a skill derived from much practice with previously described disciplines.

Liber Yod. (This was also entitled *Liber Tav* by error.) The first section of this instruction is magical, while the second and third describe classical Raja Yoga techniques.

Liber Os Abysmi. An instruction in Gnana Yoga, but directed toward demonstrating the inadequacy of the mind to resolve the basic problems of life, and thereby rising above that level.

Liber Thisharb. An instruction for developing the magical memory to recover knowledge of previous incarnations.

Liber DXXXVI. Crowley gave this practice a Greek name which is fully a line long. Gag or not, it describes a method for expanding the horizons of consciousness.

Liber Librae. A simple instruction in Karma Yoga, having been adapted without any major change from a Golden Dawn document.

Section IV. Magick

Liber O. In the most simple and direct language, without any of the turgidity or repetitiousness of the corresponding Golden Dawn material, this paper describes several practices which are the very heart and foundation of Magick.

Liber A. A method for constructing the magical instruments. It should be compared with a document in *The Golden Dawn*, vol. 3, on the construction and consecration of the elemental weapons.

Liber Resh. Here are given four adorations of the Sun to be used daily, as a means of consecrating all one's everyday activities to the Great Work.

Liber Israfel. Originally this was composed by Frater Yehi Aour (Allen Bennett) who was Crowley's first Golden Dawn mentor in the magical arts. It was adapted from versicles extrapolated from Egyptian funerary texts as an invocation of Thoth or Mercury. Crowley simply revised it, rendering it into beautiful English.

Liber XLIV: The Mass of the Phoenix. A short ritual extrapolated from *The Book of Lies*, giving a simple magical Eucharist for daily use.

Liber XXV: The Star Ruby. A modified Pentagram Ritual from *The Book of Lies.*

Liber XXXVI: The Star Sapphire. Also taken from The Book of Lies, giving another variant of the Hexagram Ritual.

Liber Samkh. An elaboration of the old Bornless Ritual or the Preliminary Invocation of the Goetia, adapted by Crowley to invoke the Holy Guardian Angel, together with his extended commentary on the ritual.

Liber V vel Reguli. Also called *The Mark of the Beast.* A later, further modified form of the Pentagram Ritual adapted to that set of ideas entertained by Crowley relative to the New Aeon and *The Book of the Law.*

The Gnostic Mass. Though this is an O.T.O. ritual extrapolated from *The Blue Equinox*, it contains much that relates to all the above and is for group working. Incidentally, it is this mass which was used, almost verbatim, by James Branch Cabell in his novel *Jurgen*, of many years ago.

Liber LXXXIX vel Chanokh. This is a brief outline published in two parts in *The Equinox*, vol. I, nos. 7 and 8, of the Enochian system of Magic derived from the skrying of Dr. John Dee and Sir Edward Kelly in Elizabethan days. The major Golden Dawn contribution has been almost entirely omitted concerning the method for forming the attributions to the squares of the Enochian Tablets and deriving pyramids from them. I would strongly recommend that these abstracts be studied in conjunction with *The Golden Dawn*, vol. 4, where this system is treated in greater detail.

Where this particular document is most valuable is in the second part, in which the Calls or Invocations in the Enochian language are to be found. It gives the magical technique of invocation of the elements and elementals. It appears nowhere else in the entire eleven volumes of *The Equinox*. This technique is in reality extrapolated from the five elemental Grade Rituals of the Golden Dawn.

Liber CCCCXVIII, being *The Vision and the Voice of the Angels of the Thirty Aethyrs*. This is a series of visions or spiritual experiences based on skrying in the thirty Aethyrs of the Enochian system. Two of them were acquired while Crowley was in Mexico in 1901, before he had gone very far on the Path. The balance of twenty-eight was obtained in the Sahara Desert where he had gone with Victor Neuburg in the year 1909. They bear evidence to the enormous spiritual and magical maturity that had developed since the earlier ones, and are consequently more coherent, profound, and sublime. It is a most significant document without parallel anywhere and serves as supreme appendix to the Enochian system.

Section V. Sex Magick

Liber A'ash vel Capricorni; Liber Cheth; and *Liber LXVI: Stellae Rubeae*. In three cryptic papers are clothed with rich symbolism, and for the untutored student may be impossible at first to understand. He will have to rely heavily on his own intuitions and whatever insights he may have developed as a result of his previous application to any or all of the methods given heretofore.

Liber DCCCXI: Energized Enthusiasm. This was originally an essay in *The Equinox*, vol. I, no. 9, but was later rendered official as a recognized instruction of the A∴A∴.

Section VI. Miscellaneous

This section includes diverse materials not included in the previous classifications, yet containing incidental elements relating to all of them.

Liber B vel Magi; Liber Porta Lvcis; Liber Tzaddi vel Hamvs Hermeticvs; Liber CCXXXI; Liber CD vel Tav; and *Liber Viarvm Viae*. Here is a group of instructions that should properly be included in any selection from The Equinox, though I cannot in all honesty believe that they add very much value to the body of instructions for which *The Equinox* is famous!

Liber CLXV: A Master of the Temple. This is an abridgement of the diary of Frater Achad, the magical pseudonym for Charles Stansfeld Jones (not to be confused with George Cecil Jones who was Crowley's mentor in the Golden Dawn period, whose magical name or initials were V.N. in the Outer Order and D.D.S. in the Inner, and were used as authorization of many of the A∴A∴ official instructions). This diary is important for several reasons, the main one being that the daily record of his various practices depicts his devotion to the Great Work. Moreover it contains comments by Crowley (who used his magical motto of O.M. 7=4) that are of the utmost value. Finally, Frater Achad made some important contributions to the understanding of *Liber AL vel Legis* which are recognized and given credit in the long commentary on that book. Achad also wrote some books on the Qabalah which deviated from the basic pattern of both Crowley and the Golden Dawn, which thus led ultimately to the separation of these two men–a very sad event.

Liber LXXI. Madame Blavatsky wrote a small book entitled *The Voice of the Silence*, which since her day became acknowledged as a mystical and devotional classic. Crowley, using his motto of O.M., has commented at considerable length on this classic. I have long felt that it deserves a broader circulation among occult students who appear to have no awareness of the fact that there exists this erudite and extraordinary commentary to Blavatsky's work.

Some general note need to be made concerning the relationship of Blavatsky and Crowley. The latter made much of the fact that he was born in the year that Blavatsky founded the original Theosophical Society. In this writings there will occasionally be found a note of derision about both Madame Blavatsky and the Theosophists. Be that as it may, later on he became far more respectful, and then enunciated the doctrine that she was his predecessor–rather like John the Baptist preceding Jesus. In *Magick without Tears* there will be found some letters on *The Three Schools of Magick* in which this doctrine is enunciated at great length. (Remember that Crowley believed that his publication of *The Equinox* was the first serious work on occultism since Blavatsky wrote Isis Unveiled.)

I must confess that I find this set of ideas rather preposterous. The first and most important reason is that Blavatsky was altogether opposed to the average Westerner practicing any of the occult arts. This was one of her most fundamental statements as anyone familiar with the history of the Theosophical Society must soon realize. On the other hand, Crowley strongly recommended the total abandonment of intellectual speculation of any sort and the resort to the practice of Yoga and Magick in order to permit the illumination of the Ruach or Lower Manas by a higher order of being or consciousness. The opposition is so blatant and so well defined that I fail to see how Crowley could insist that there was any kind of relationship between Blavatsky and himself, when in fact, their respective occult attitudes are so wholly different–antipodal.

Section VII. Reviews

This last section contains some of the book reviews and profiles that ran like fire through the pages of *The Equinox*. They are included in this collection of documents not merely because I have obtained so much personal pleasure from them throughout the years, but because, in addition, the student can glean much that is of value magically. Every now and again you stumble across a sentence that packs a tremendous wallop. They also reveal with startling clarity much of the basic attitude of Crowley toward almost everything.

The profiles I have always found fascinating. In almost every issue of *The Equinox* there was either a review of some book written by Arthur Edward Waite, or a longer profile that has had me in stitches again and again. If the reader has not ready anything of Waite, much of the stinging nature of these articles will be lost on him. Therefore I would strongly recommend that the reader first peruse any book authored by Waite. Only recently, just to refresh my memory, I glanced through two of them, *The Holy Grail* and *The Brotherhood of the Rosy Cross*. Altogether apart from their content which is sometimes difficult to determine, the literary style of Waite comes through loud and clear. It is turgid, pompous and pretentious. One realizes anew how utterly right Crowley was in his critical evaluation of this occult writer. Waite is practically unreadable.

Other profiles are satirical. One of them, *Shadowy Dill-Waters* lampoons W.B. Yeats who is called Weary Willie. There was much bad blood existing between these two poets, which dates back to the Golden Dawn revolt when they faced each other from opposite sides of the fence.

Much the same has to be said of Algernon Blackwood. Whenever any book of his was reviewed by Aleister Crowley, the opportunity was taken to deride him thoroughly and I must say unjustly. Blackwood was another of those writers who was in the Golden Dawn.

There is another profile which takes G.K. Chesterton to task. Long prior to the writing of his particular profile Crowley and Chesterton had engaged in a continual battle. Chesterton had reviewed some of Crowley's early books, and being an apologist for Catholicism, had expressed some displeasure over Crowley's devotion to Egyptian Gods. Chesterton ridiculed some of their names. Crowley replied to this criticism by calling Chesterton's attention to the fact that Yah and Yahweh of the Bible were no less ridiculous. Thus there were frequent skirmishes between these two men. *The Equinox* profile, though not mentioning this particular history, nonetheless was predicated emotionally on what had transpired between them.

Another profile is a melange of praise for and severe criticism of G.B. Shaw. Almost more than any of the others, this one vividly reveals Crowley's attitude to literature. While he respects the cleverness of Shaw, the fact that there is no trace in the latter's writing of any glimmering of ecstasy is stressed more than anything else. It is for this that he reprimands Shaw severely.

Omissions

Running through all the ten volumes is a serial narrative entitled *The Temple of Solomon the King*. The first four pasts were written by Captain J.F.C. Fuller. His literary style can be recognized by its floridity, its enthusiasm, and by an overt attempt to appear profound, occult and recondite. The remaining parts were contributed by Crowley himself. The serial is a biographical account of Crowley's spiritual attainment, from the early days of his entry into the Golden Dawn, the great revelation of *The Book of the Law* which he received in Cairo, to his final passage through the Abyss. For that illumination, he modestly chose a Latino motto V.V.V.V.V. which, rendered into decent English, means "In my lifetime I have conquered the Universe by the force of Truth."

However fascinating and important this serial is, I have decided to omit it from *Gems from the Equinox* for several reasons. First of all, Crowley's own autobiography *The Confessions* (New York: Hill and Wang, 1970) has appeared. My own biographical study of Crowley, *The Eye in the Triangle*, has been published also. These, in my estimation, supersede *The Temple of Solomon the King*.

I have it on rumor that someone else will publish the latter, and I have recommended that with this serial the editor in question should include with it the following material from *The Equinox: The Electric Silence*, an idealized biographical and symbolical story of Aleister Crowley's quest; *John St. John*, an account of a short retirement in the heart of Paris, leading to an illumination; and *Across the Gulf*, a fantastic account of a previous incarnation in Egypt.

I have also omitted the instructions on Geomancy and the Tarot. Since both of these were original Golden Dawn materials, they were republished by me years ago in my book *The Golden Dawn*, based on documents circulating within the Order.

The Equinox instruction on Geomancy is not complete or workable the *modus operandi* is most inadequately delineated, and above all, the geomantic sigils of the planetary rulers had been deleted, which really robs the method of its divinatory efficacy. Both of these are given in *The Golden Dawn*.

In Crowley's Tarot instruction he had changed the counting formula for some of the cards, primarily to accord with that verse in *Liber AL vel Legis* which says: "My number is 11, as all their numbers who are of us." Not that this really makes much difference. The only thing that is required of any system is coherency and consistency, and so long as it is understood that 11 is an intrinsic part of that system it will work. But that number had nothing to do with the Golden Dawn system as such.

Incidentally, it should be clearly understood that this document has nothing whatsoever to do with Crowley's masterpiece of later years, *The Tarot of the Egyptians* (New York: Samuel Weiser, 1969). This is an entirely different piece of writing and artistry.

The Equinox, vol. I, no. 8, contains *Liber D: Sepher Sephiroth*. This is such a large tome, containing as it does a vast collection of names in English and Hebrew together with their numerical values or Gematrias, with many words from the Zohar and the Bible, that I feel it would really be too bulky to include in this book. I have decided therefore to exclude it altogether.

However, I strongly suggest that the two independent publishers of the other important Qabalistic work of Crowley's *Liber 777* get together and between them reproduce *Sepher Sephiroth* as a companion volume to *Liber 777*. It should contain a brief essay on how too use it.

Liber DCCCCLXIII is to be found in *The Equinox*, vol. I, no. 3. It was originally written by Captain J.F.C. Fuller, with only the short prefatory note having been written by Crowley. It is a lengthy document, lyrical certainly in spots, but wordy and repetitious. A sample reads:

> O Thou Dragon-prince of the air, that art drunk on the blood of the sunsets! I adore Thee, Evoe! I adore Thee, IAO!
>
> O Thou sparkling wine-cup of light, whose foaming is the hearts' blood of the stars! I adore Thee, Evoe! I adore Thee, IAO!
>
> O Thou frail bluebell of moonlight, that art lost in the gardens of the stars! I adore Thee, Evoe! I adore Thee, IAO!

A few are splendid and exhilarating. Nearly a hundred pages of such adorations, despite a few changes and variations, become rather monotonous. Thus its omission here.

In *The Blue Equinox* Crowley published *Liber LXV: The Book of the Heart Girt with a Serpent*. This is one of a handful of sublime mystical books written by Crowley in the heyday of his early spiritual attainment. They were then published by him in a small, private edition, printed on Japanese vellum with gold margins or borders and bound in vellum. They are among the grandest and finest things he has ever penned.

The Sangreal Foundation (Dallas: 1969) has republished *Liber LXV* together with *Liber VII vel Lapidis Lazuli* and *Liber DCCCXIII vel Ararita* under the title of *The Holy Books*, but this was my error and I assume full responsibility for this piece of carelessness.

Two others of these so-called holy books are included in the *Gems from The Equinox*. *Liber AL Legis* is included here (despite the fact that a cheap paperback edition has recently seen the light of day [North Hollywood: Xeno Publications, 1968] because according to Crowley it is the foundation of his system. The other is *Liber LXI*, the History Lection, giving Crowley's version of the origins of the Golden Dawn and thus of his own A∴A∴.

The only one that has thus been omitted is *Liber Trigrammaton*. It may sound naive and presumptuous to say that it means precious little to me. And because it does not appear in any volume of *The Equinox*, I have decided not to go outside of those volumes.

In *The Equinox*, vol. I, no. I, there is an obscure alchemical piece entitled *The Chymical Jousting of Brother Peradua*. Written by Captain J.F.C. Fuller, it is as usual ebullient and effervescent, and almost conveys the impression of being informative. Actually it says nothing and is merely a literary tour de force.

I would suggest that this piece of virtuosity was an attempt to copy an earlier paper by Crowley called *Ambrosii Magi Hortus Rosarum* (circa 1902) containing among other matters some obscure erotic references which can be inferred by a close scrutiny of the margin notes. It is interesting and amusing, bearing all the earmarks of a Crowley effort to imitate the classical *Chymical Marriage of Christian Rosencreutz*. It is here omitted.

Several other omissions should be mentioned for the sake of completeness. One is *The Key to The Mysteries* written by Eliphas Levi and translated by Crowley, published in *The Equinox*, vol. I, no. 10. It has since appeared in book form under the auspices of Riders of London.

Crowley thought this a magnificent piece of writing and used it as his thesis for the grade of Adeptus Exemptus. I cannot say I find this, or really any other writing from the French schools of occultism, of much value and can only assume that Crowley admired it because he was Eliphas Levi in his previous incarnation–or so he said. It is, however, inferior to other of the contents of *The Equinox* reproduced here.

Another omission is *The Rites of Eleusis*, found in the supplement to *The Equinox*, vol. I, no 6. These rituals were written for public performance during the Equinox heydey, serving as a means for demonstrating the violin virtuosity of Leila Waddell, Crowley's mistress at that time, the dance-to-exhaustion technique of Victor Neuburg, and a large number of poems written by Crowley. The reviews written at that time indicate that the Rites were quite a performance and were well received. But I see little in them of exceptional value to the present-day student of Magick, who as I have previously noted, is not particularly fond of poetry. Under these circumstances, most of the Rites in poetic form would be wholly lost on him.

The four essays entitled *The Herb Dangerous*, published in the first four volumes of *The Equinox*, are so good–from the point of view of both style and content–that I extrapolated them from *The Equinox* and republished them under the title *Roll Away the Stone* (St. Paul: Llewellyn Publications, 1968). I wrote a lengthy introduction relating them to the current drug scene. There is thus no need to reissue them in this edition.

Another worthwhile essay in *The Equinox*, vol. I, no. I, entitled *The Soldier! and the Hunchback?* is omitted here. I think that all essays of Crowley, including *Berashith, Eleusis*, and *Science and Buddhism*, etc., should be gathered together and issued at a later date in a single volume when the public has begun to appreciate his prose and his intellectual acumen.

There are a few other omissions but minor in character. If not mentioned in this list, they do nothing one way or another for the basic material reproduced here.

At one time I thought that the A∴A∴ and the O.T.O. had ceased to exist with Crowley's demise in 1947; however, I am now informed otherwise. There is a very active branch of both Orders in Switzerland under aggressive and wise leadership. It republishes some of *The Equinox* material in German translation and issues a monthly periodical of its own called the *Oriflamme*.

In this country, as in England, eruptions of activity come to my attention every now and again, indicating that some of the original members continue quietly the work laid down by Crowley. Perhaps it is also true in other parts of the world.

Currently I am not a member of any Order. But if any reader wishes to be put in contact with some of the branches mentioned above, a note addressed to me in care of the publisher will be duly forwarded.

With this publication of *Gems from The Equinox*, I almost feel like repeating the Golden Dawn speech that I used on the last page of *My Rosicrucian Adventure*: "Let us work, therefore, my brethren and effect righteousness, because the Night cometh when no man shall labour."

This promise or foreboding seems more applicable to the very near future than it did thirty years ago. However, I need to modify it a little. I do feel my work is done at this time and I pray the Gods will now release me from the preoccupation of presenting the work of Aleister Crowley that has lain heavily on me for so long a period of time. With the publication of this book, my obligation to him, whatever it was, is surely fulfilled. Thus I can pass from labor to refreshment, to concern myself with other things.

Israel Regardie

March 31, 1970
Studio City, California

HEALING ENERGY PRAYER & RELAXATION
Preface by Israel Regardie
New Falcon Publishing, First Edition, 1982

Countless books have already been written and published on prayer and relaxation. Why the need for another?

Many years devoted to varied forms of psychotherapy, as well as prolonged exposure to mysticism and allied topics, are the main factors that have led me to a rather different approach to this topic.

In the course of my professional life, what struck me vividly was that when people were enabled to shuffle off the unconscious armor of gross muscular tension, thus achieving a never-before-experienced delight and pleasure in the relaxation of psyche and soma, entirely new attitudes towards religion and prayer spontaneously developed. They needed no orientation, no preparation, no coaching. It was just there. And a whole new life of fervor, inspiration and prayer made its appearance. Not prayer in the conventional institutionalized form, but an intimacy with Life and Love that are intense, devout, springing from wells deep within the psyche.

It would seem that once the armoring had been dissipated, in the true Reichian sense of the term, vital energies which had been locked up or anchored in the muscular hypertension, found their own kind of outlet. Someone long ago said man is a religious animal. The release of these bio-energies brought with them the confirmation of this statement. Some had never before been religious in their lives–others had been raised in the formal religions of today but had become wholly disenchanted, rebelling harshly against them. After thus rejecting the faith of their childhood, suddenly they found themselves developing new and fascinating insights into those early faiths. Even the old prayer and hymns once memorized by rote gradually became alive and revealed new meanings and new stirrings within. They learned spontaneously to pray.

It was not learned in any ordinary sense. And it most assuredly was not something they acquired from me. It was a hard and fast rule of mine never to talk to patients about my metaphysical or occult faith. Most never knew I had written about the subject. Only if they had previously encountered my writings did I acknowledge with some hesitation an interest in these matters. Even then it was sparing, a begrudging acknowledgement–deliberately adopted so that their own growth and development would not be prejudicially affected by me.

So it was all the more gratifying and exciting when, as therapy progressed and their own energies were released, their own native "religious" sense began to emerge. It introduced them to an entirely new way of life, of thinking and feeling and aspiring. It is with all this in mind, that this book is offered–sincerely hoping that the general reader too may find his own path to the heights of attainment. That he too may discover God (whatever he may understand by this), or the Universal Life Energy, in ways that are peculiar and special to him.

My best wishes and blessings, for whatever they may be worth, go forth with this hope.

May 11, 1982
Arizona

THE HOLY BOOKS
Preface by Israel Regardie
Sangreal Printing, 1972

After years of turmoil, strict discipline and rigorous application of diverse techniques, Aleister Crowley finally reached the mystical heights. It was in 1907, or shortly thereafter, upon his return from the southern borders of China, that he coined the magical mottos "*Vi Verum Universum Vivus Vici*"–"I have conquered the universe by the force of truth." It was his personal expression to the most sublime mystical attainment that he could envision at that time.

The first of the three mellifluous texts he wrote under this pseudonym was *Liber VII*, celebrating his difficult crossing of the Abyss and so arriving at Spiritual puberty. Its poem is a lyrical paean of simplicity, pure devotion and ecstasy. *Liber LXV* succeeded it as a more mature expression of his spiritual understanding. Its beauty and delicacy are haunting experiences never to be forgotten. Probably much later, he wrote *Liber Ararita* where he made use of the Qabalistic Tree of Life in several different ways, posing thesis against antithesis, uniting them, and transcending them by negation in Zen-like manner.

Crowley could never quite bring himself to discuss these exalted masterpieces. Though he did write a commentary on at least two of them, in the face of these ineffable songs he became dumb-struck. They are gems in the diadem of his spiritual achievement, having no counterpart whatsoever in the literature of mystical experience.

Their value lies in the extraordinary ability of the writer to facilitate identification with his own dynamic experience. By sympathetic induction, the student could be helped to participate directly in the same spiritual experience through which Crowley had just recently passed. His original recommendation to students was that at least one chapter of each of these books be memorized at different stages of development; I can recommend lovingly no less.

March 20, 1969
Studio City, California

FOREWORDS
by Israel Regardie

THE MIDDLE PILLAR
Foreword and Chapter One
by Israel Regardie
New Falcon Publishing, First Edition, 2018

This book was completed in February 1936, anterior to the writing of *The Art of True Healing*, whilst I was still resident in London. My point of view since that time has undergone considerable revision, mostly by way of extension. I could easily have altered the text to conform to my present thinking on such matters as the importance of the art of Relaxation in relation to the welfare both of body and mind. But I have refrained from doing so since such alteration would interfere with the integrity and continuity of the book as an expression of myself at that time.

For me *The Middle Pillar* marks a certain stage of psychological development. I prefer not to tamper with temporal markings and inner milestones. Such a stage may correspond with that of other people who may thus find it of no little value, I may dilate at greater length and freedom upon the important implications of Relaxation and Psychological Analysis insofar as they have bearing upon spiritual development and unfoldment.

Israel Regardie

January 31st, 1938
New York City

CHAPTER ONE

To me one of the most significant and extraordinary characteristics of modern thought is the widespread circulation of books on psychology in its various branches. There is a general interest in matters dealing with the mind–especially with that aspect of the hinterland of the mind which has been named of the Unconscious for want of better words and also because its realm at the moment is so ambiguous to us. There could hardly be an educated individual who has not some slight degree of acquaintance with this analytical psychology. Even if this familiarity ran only to an acquaintance with several of the more commonly employed *cliches*–such as libido, the unconscious, conflicts and resistances, neuroses and complexes–that in itself would be indicative of a phenomenon which surely has occurred seldom before in the history of civilised thought.

To meet this widespread interest in matters psychological, a number of books have been written to give the general reader some notion of that peculiar world with which it is the province of the analyst to deal. Quite a number of these are extremely informative, providing a very sane and balanced view of the subject. On the one hand, as is inevitable, there is a large number which might just as well have remained unwritten. One of the most curious misconceptions promulgated by some of these latter is the fact that analytical psychology–and here I use this term in its widest sense to cover the various schools inaugurated by Freud, Jung, Adler, etc.–is a thing quite apart, and that the one thing which stamped our ancestors as barbarians and savages was their utter lack of acquaintance with psycho-therapy. It would be totally absurd for anyone to minimise all that has been achieved by modern psychology, due to the efforts of such astute investigators as Freud and Jung. But it is abundantly clear that their protagonists–psychological extremists–go entirely too far in disclaiming the intelligence and insight of our predecessors. For the facts are, as but little research indicates, that so far from being ignorant of analytical psychology, the ancients, and particularly those of the East and hither East, had evolved a highly complex and elaborate scheme not only of analysis, but also of spiritual development and synthesis.

Some orthodox die-hards may question the relationship of modern psychology with discredited oriental and archaic techniques for the unfolding of man's higher or spiritual nature. In practice, however, such a relationship does indubitably exist. It is a fact of clinical and consulting-room experience. For, during the course of a protracted analysis, the cruder and more superficial unconscious levels having been uncovered and moral conflicts resolved, symbols and theme-motifs of a religious or spiritual nature do make their entry by way of dream, intuition, and by direct apprehension. Not only is this so, but they exert a potent influence on the entire personality, producing integrity, a new and more equilibrated attitude towards life, and an unification of the various strata of consciousness which collectively we call man.

What modern psychology has quite possibly accomplished is an advance over the efforts of our predecessors in the way of a cathartic technique. Moreover, because of modern devices, the methods of analytical psychology have been brought nearer to the understanding and convenience of the ordinary man of the street. In the past, the techniques of attainment, Mysticism, Magic, and Yoga, or by whatever name such systems were denoted, were always several removes from the ken of the average individual.

The psychologies of the past may be summarised by the use of the words Yoga and Magic. The subject of Yoga has already been excellently dealt with by several able and competent writers, requiring therefore but little mention here. Such a book as *Yoga and Western Psychology* by Geraldine Coster must certainly take its place historically as a genuine and first-rate contribution to the progress of analytical psychology. There is also the compilation of the Buddhist Lodge *Concentration and Meditation*, a handbook on that subject of great merit. A number of modern psychologists have also examined the subject of Yoga and meditation as a whole, and have found much that is sympathetic to and explanatory of their own systems. And furthermore, the mystical systems posit a goal and a general schema which expand the rather hazy and indeterminate character of a very large part of our psycho-therapeutic systems.

Analytical Psychology and Magic comprise in my estimation two halves or aspects of a single technical system. Just as the body and mind are not two separate units, but are simply the dual manifestations of an interior dynamic "something" so psychology and Magic comprise similarly a single system whose goal is the integration of the human personality. Its aim is to unify the different departments and functions of man's being, to bring into operation those which previously for various reasons were latent. Incidentally, its technique is such that neurotic symptoms which were too insistent upon expression either become eliminated or toned down by a process of equilibration.

It will be obvious, then, that by Magic we are not considering a theatrical craft or jugglery–and certainly not that mediaeval superstition which was the child of ignorance begotten by fear and terror. These definitions should be expunged from our thinking. For centuries magic has been quite erroneously associated with such pathologies as witchcraft and demonolatry due to the duplicity of charlatans and the reticence of its own so-called authorities. Even today, the custodians of this knowledge, harassed by personal problems and more especially by their own power complex are still adamant in their traditional refusal to circulate a more accurate description of the nature of Magic. Possibly even they have lost all understanding of its principles. No wonder this misconception exists. With the exception of very few works which have attracted the attention of but a fractional part of the reading public, little has been written to act as a definitive exposition of what Magic really is. Inasmuch as something of the nature of modern Psychology is at least partially understood by a fair section of the educated world, were it said that Magic is akin to and concerns itself with that same subjective realm of psychology, some notion of its character and objectives come within hailing distance.

So far as the average man or aspirant to Magic is concerned, unquestionably the analytic technique should comprise the first stage of the routine employed in spiritual development. For until one understands himself according to that peculiarly penetrating light which Psychology has thrown upon our motives, he cannot hope to bring effectively into operation the dormant side of his nature. And lest anyone casually dismiss this desirable self-knowledge as a goal easily attained to or, it may be, already obtained, one can only utter a solemn warning that this is not so simple as at first sight seems. That self-knowledge is necessary to the pursuit of Magic is self-evident. At once we are faced at the portal by guardians armed to the teeth. Such queries confront us as: suppose the interest in spiritual culture were motivated by a desire to escape from the turbulence of physical life? What if one's stubbornly defended point of view were only an elaborate rationalisation to conceal the sense of insecurity, the dull but insistent ache of inferiority? These are quite often the unrecognised factors which compel refuge in the religious avocation–even in various branches of science too. The search for, and quite often assumed discovery of some paternal-like God or a testy senior after the fashion of Jehovah, frequently has its origins in an adolescent rejection of the father. This deliberately forgotten, has become so deep, that the inner psychic necessity for the authority and affection of the father is unconsciously projected outwards into a terrifying and awe-inspiring deity. Discernment of the true motives and conduct and attitudes towards life is, therefore, an absolute essential. This accomplished, then may be examined that other side of the medallion which is man's own psyche.

As a practical system, Magic is concerned not so much with analysis as with bringing into operation the creative and intuitive parts of man. A psychological technique can never be a wholly integrative one until it accepts this spiritual side of man and assists the analysand in the recognition of or acquaintance with its activity. At this moment, the treatment of these matters remains almost entirely within the domain of Magic alone. Fully does it recognise the necessity for integration. Not only does it accept and recommend the results of analysis, but it proceeds still further. If analysis aims at the acceptance of the Unconsciousness, then Magic may be said to be a technique for realising the deeper levels of the Unconscious. These are levels of power and realisation whose value we can but dimly grasp through contemplation of religious figures of the past. Buddha, Jesus, Krishna, St. Francis, and a host of others are instances of such illuminated men–of individuals who have striven, all in different ways, to know themselves and attain to a realisation of their true divine nature. If we wish to use the techniques they employed, they were many, however, they are identical in spirit called devotion, meditation, and contemplation. They are fundamental with what we now propose to discuss as Magic.

In the latter, however, the entire process of attainment has been systematised and developed almost into an exact science, having as its foundation the discovery of Godhead. While there may be very few in life who can attain to the full realisation of their divine origin and nature, yet for all of us there is some value of Magic, some degree of fulfilment or attainment available. There is none so small as cannot employ it to some good and noble end. None so great as cannot better himself more efficient to cope with and understand life and the world both about and within him. These are objectives which, notwithstanding the magnitudes of their vision, are within the reach of every man.

It is not yet the moment to enter into a disquisition on the intricacies of magical ritual. But in order to expound fundamental psychological and spiritual principles it is necessary to refer to what are known technically as the Two Pillars. Half-way between the East and West, and North and South, in a properly instituted Temple are placed two upright pillars. One of these is coloured white, the other black. These pieces of lodge furniture are emblematical of the two opposites functioning in the diverse operations of nature. Just as the Temple represents in miniature the whole of life by which we may ever be confronted, or, rather, the manifold parts of our own inner nature, so these two pillars symbolise some aspect of these phenomena. They represent light and darkness, heat and cold. In man, they stand for love and hate, joy and pain, mind and emotion, life and death, sleeping and waking. Every pair of opposites conceivable to the human mind find their representation in the implication of these two pillars.

Now one of the most important ideas communicated to the student of Magic, in his ceremonial initiation when he is led from one station to another, is that an extreme leaning either to one or the other of the opposites is a very dangerous thing. It is unwise to swing to opposite poles of life's pendulum. "Unbalanced power is the ebbing away of life. Unbalanced mercy is but weakness and the fading out of the will. Unbalanced severity is cruelty and the barrenness of mind."

Were we to change the terminology of the speech, instead of the word 'Mercy', we might substitute 'emotion', or 'generosity' or 'love'; for 'Severity' we may substitute 'power'. 'rational side of us', or 'justice' or 'tyranny'. Either of these qualities when carried to an extreme, unmodified by the other, is conducive to an unhealthy state of psyche. Thus it is, that in so religiously authoritative a book as the Bhagavad-Gita, which some consider one of the finest pieces of devotional and philosophical literature yet penned, we find it stated "Be free from the pairs of opposites."

The whole of life–it is in fact the law of Nature itself– seems to be dominated by these extremes or opposites. "Two contending forces and one which unites them eternally. Two basal angles of the triangle and one which forms the apex. Such is the origin of creation; it is the Triad of Life." Only a little reflection will convince the reader of the truth of this theorum. Until we have acquired wisdom and understanding, we swing during the seventy year span of our lives between self-esteem and self-disgust, from an exaggerated estimation of our fellows to their utter and final condemnation. Age, it is true, does bring moderation and temperance with it. But were this more balanced attitude towards life cultivated, taught or adopted earlier or before middle age set in, how much more efficient could we not be, and what could we not achieve? The technique under consideration consists primarily in the conscious reconciliation of opposing forces. It is this which has been called the development of the Golden Flower.

Before proceeding further, it is a very interesting piece of speculation to consider the trinities of various religions. Most of them resolve themselves when all theological argument and intellectual quibbling are eliminated, into some such relationship as Father, Mother and Son. Osiris, Isis and Horus are an excellent example. This is true of the Christian system where, upon careful consideration we find the Holy Ghost defined as a feminine aspect of godhead. And in the Hebrew Qabalah we have the Trinity on the Tree of Life of CHESED Mercy, GEVURAH Might and TIPHARAS Equilibrium or Beauty. Co-relating this latter triad with traditional symbolism, CHESED is masculine, referred to Jupiter, a paternal wisdom symbol. GEVURAH, feminine, is attributed to Mars, indicative of great power. One alchemical aphorism expresses this duality in the words "Man is peace and Woman is power." Bearing all these in mind, we conclude that as CHESED represents the Father and GEVURAH the Mother, so TIPHARAS which is Beauty, is the reconciler between them. Interestingly enough, TIPHARAS is referred to the Sun, and corresponds to the third member of the theological trinity, the Son.

Looking at these trinities as so many expressions of psychological fact–that is, as previously defined, as factors active within the psyche itself–we are struck by the similarity of the religious point of view with the idea of the Middle Way. It is the pursuit of this middle path which leads to self-conquest and the steady growth of the Golden Flower, the wakening of the imprisoned soul within.

The Father and Mother may be said to correspond to the two Pillars of the Temple, to the two extremes or opposites.

In this sense they are the tendencies exhibited by all the phenomena of Nature. They are the extremes of spirit and matter, love and hate, life and death, ebb and flow, systole and diastole. Nature itself is the embodiment of the two extremes, the two opposites of the Trinity. Man, unenlightened man, one in whom neither wisdom nor understanding has been brought to birth, likewise fashions his life in the way of these two extremes. Or rather, these extremes fashion in his life for him. For he is, as though by compulsion, driven by some external force he knows not of, between the poles of extreme love and hate, swinging from kindness and maudlin generosity to bursts of uncontrolled anger, hate and meanness. His actions, almost without a single exception, are so many semi-hysterical flights from pole to pole of his emotions. He is, as it were, under the dominion of the Father and the Mother.

To the student of the psyche, to the one who seeks wisdom and the knowledge of his higher Self, the counsel has always been given to avoid the opposites. His task is to refrain from the compulsion of extreme actions.

In certain schools of Magic, where the rites of initiation were celebrated by Adepts who at one time thoroughly understood the technique they employed, initiation ceremonies depicted the burial of the higher Self and its rebirth by means of a technical system of Magic and Meditation. Therein, the higher Self was always represented by some sacred figure of the major religions–a man who was nearly always shown as the Son of God. The essence of the ethical injunctions of these systems was to develop the Son within. "Unless Christ be born in you…" "Look within; thou are Buddha." I do not believe these images could possibly have reference to any historical individual we know of. But rather I surmise these refer to the gradual bringing into conscious operation of a spiritual point of view, of an equilibrated attitude towards life, an attitude not exclusively directed to any extreme. Recognising the polarity of life, such a point of view sought to steer a middle way between the tortuous and extreme activity of Nature. It is the way of the Reconciler, of keeping to the path between the two Pillars, that balanced and harmonious position in which the candidates of the ancient initiation systems found themselves at the major crisis and climax of their initiation. This is the technique of bringing to birth the golden Sun of TIPHARAS, the Sun of beauty and harmony who is the third person of the trinity. Thus it is that one system nowadays conceives of the Great Work as partaking of the recognition of the Crowned and Conquering Child Horus–he who, while partaking necessarily of the nature of both the Father and the Mother, is simultaneously an entirely different and unique being. Through the result of the union of opposing forces, his nature tends to a new viewpoint in the conquest of life. For the Father and Mother are "those forces whose reconciliation is the key of life."

To illustrate in another way the import of this concept, let us describe it from a practical and physical point of view. One of the major inconveniences which afflicts a large portion of mankind is constipation. In many instances of this disorder, no organic disturbance exists at all; the trouble being principally a functional one. (Though it must be here interpolated that even if it were organic, there is sufficient psychological evidence to indicate that this likewise may ensue from an identical series of causes.) Very often, this malady does not respond to any kind of medical treatment. It is not uncommon for patients to testify that they have been recommended massage, surgical operations, drugs, nature cure and all the other types of cures. In spite of these the illness persists unchanged. Enquiry elicits that there is, frequently, a conscious conflict between two courses of conduct. More often than not, however, the real seat of the conflict is not in consciousness, at all, but exists in a far deeper level of mind, in the Unconscious. It was probably around puberty that an already existent conflict developed such acuteness and severity as to require for the psychic safety of the ego to be repressed completely out of sight.

From this, we might conclude–and there is some psychological evidence to this end–that the conflict is one between the instincts and social dictates. That is, because of parental training there is a blind refusal to recognise the necessity for the proper and legitimate expression of the instincts. It is a denial of one side of the personality, a denial without justification or reason. It is as though, while admiring the beauty and form of the lotus, we wished not to be reminded of the slimy source where grow the roots of the plant, and therefore cut the stalk right through, severing the flower from its necessary root. This cutting of the lotus stalk has its counterpart in human minds, many of us having been cut off from our roots. For this denial of the instinctual life, in which the conscious existence after all has its roots, and this persistent repression, cause some degree of dissociation. That is, a severance of the integrity and unity of the psyche. The psychosis, if sufficiently intense and prolonged, produces symptoms of various sorts ranging from lack of vitality, irritability, constipation, and a host of other physical and nervous disorders.

With such a problem, there is but one logical method of attack. It is to recognise quite clearly that the physical symptoms are the results of an internal conflict between the needs of the body and the self-sufficiency or cowardice of the mind. It is a conflict between the necessity to the expression of emotion and feeling, and the imperious urge of the ego to escape from a vulnerable constituent of its nature, that principle which at one time had been susceptible to hurt and injury. With the frank recognition of the conflict, one should endeavour to recollect the events of his early childhood, bringing up as many memories as possible of that period, experiencing neither shame nor remorse at his discoveries. Confronting these memories with the knowledge that as an adult in whom is the light of reason, he understands that his mature mind can dissipate the infantile emotion connected with early experiences, in which shame or inferiority or insecurity was felt. In this way, he links and applies mind to emotion, thus avoiding within him the uncontrolled play of the opposites. Their existence is neither denied nor frustrated. This is a vital point to be understood. No denial or rejection should be countenanced of what manifestly is an actual fact, no stubborn refusal to admit and accept a part of his own nature. As we have seen, the denial of any function of the self leads to dissociation, and the latter results in nervous and physical disorders.

Face the fact that at one time there was a denial of one phase of life, and thus accept the conflict. Accept it, knowing that so long as we remain human, these conflicts are bound to be our lot. In our present stage of evolution, they are part and parcel of human nature, and so cannot be avoided. But what can be eliminated is the ignorant attitude so often adopted towards them. For these opposites, the two Pillars of the Temple, their magical images or prototypes, represent "those eternal forces betwixt which the equilibrium of the universe dependeth. Those forces whose reconciliation is the Key of Life, whose separation is evil and death." This, then, is the solution to conflict. They must be reconciled.

Let me recapitulate. There must be the clear recognition of the conflict. Its exact nature must be analysed and faced, and its presence accepted in all its implications.

One must endeavour to bring up into consciousness, so far as the capabilities of the mind permit, all the memories of childhood. In a word, he should attempt to perform a species of what is called in the Buddhist system the *Sammasati* meditation. This consists in a cultivation and rigid examination of memory. The idea involved here is not that these recollections in themselves are worth anything, but that raising them up to surface releases a great deal of tension associated with early experiences. There is often a tying up of nervous energy in childhood experiences, in trivial events which are allowed to be forgotten and to sink into unconsciousness. But this forgetfulness does not overcome the shock of nervous exhaustion connected with them. On the contrary, they set up what are called resistances–resistances to the flow of life and vitality from the primitive and vital layers of the Unconscious level.

"What matters," remarks Georg Groddeck the brilliant German physician-psychologist, "is not to make conscious anything at all of the Unconscious, but to relieve what is imprisoned, and in so doing it is by no means rare for the repressed material to sink into the depths instead of coming into consciousness... What is decisive in the success of treatment is the removal of resistance."

Beginning with the actual events of the day upon which the reader determines to commence this exercise, the meditation should gradually extend its field of vision until ultimately the events and occurrences of the earliest years are brought into the light of day. The technique is principally one of the training of the mind to think backwards. Difficult though at first it may seem, practice leads the student slowly and gradually to facility in the art of remembering. The facts of memory confronted fearlessly, without shame and discomforture, the resistance to the flow of vitality between the various levels of consciousness is broken down, restoring physical, nervous and spiritual health.

As the childhood memories are exposed, the student will see for himself in what way the conflict now bothering him came into manifestation. Since by definition a neurosis is a maladaptation of the psyche to life itself, by this process of remembering he will see in what way he failed to respond properly to the phenomena of his existence.

Realising this, and recognising thoroughly the nature of his conflict, he must now endeavour to ignore it. More accurately a more positive attitude should be adopted. He must develop in an entirely new direction. It must be remembered, however, and this is important, that to ignore any symptom of conflict as manifested in mind or body, is dangerous until the conflict in question has been recognised and accepted. The unconditional acceptance almost invariably acts as its resolution. Any other attitude constitutes an escape.

The escape mechanism is that so frequently adopted by the neurotic and must be avoided. It is the way of the coward. To face the conflict is to rob it and its consequences of crippling fear. Honesty with oneself acts as a catharsis. One finds himself imbued with a new courage and greater ability to face one's problem in an entirely new and more practicable way. Given the recognition of the conflict causing constipation, the symptom itself may be severely ignored, relying upon the bowel after the lapse of some days to recommence functioning of its own accord. The conflict and the warring between the two sides of the psyche, tied a knot as it were in consciousness preventing the perfect functioning of the whole. The immediate result of this is an impediment in the free movement of nervous energy in the body-mind system, causing stasis in that part of the system having a relationship or correspondence with the factors concerned in the conflict.

Occult theory as we have it from tradition may be extremely useful here. With some degree of practical experience, we could easily discover the precise nature of the original conflict by a consideration of that part of the organism to the symptoms of which our attention is attracted. For example, consider one troubled by nephritis. One of the most significant aspects of the magical tradition is Astrology. In this latter science the kidneys are referred to the operation of the planet Venus. As we know from mythology, Venus is the deity concerned with love, feeling and emotion. We would surmise therefore that in the event that the love or emotional life of an individual has been frustrated or repressed to such a point where the psyche finally refused to continue living whilst hampered by such a neurosis, some expression of that frustration could be transferred to the neighborhood of the kidneys. Were the frustration complete and devastating to the psyche, it is not impossible that we should find a cancer–the symptom par excellence of the death-wish, the so-called suicide complex indicative of a division in the psyche's integrity.

Moreover, we could proceed a step further. We might enquire as to whether the affliction were on the right or left, remembering the Qabalistic definition of the Left Pillar as the side of Mercy, and that on the Right as the Pillar of Severity.

"Unbalanced mercy is weakness and the fading out of the will. Unbalanced severity is cruelty and the barrenness of mind."

Enquiry might elicit the fact that an afflicted left kidney were symptomatic of one who had been afraid to taste life to the full. Or on the other hand, out of sheer compensation, had lived so completely as to have over-indulged. The right kidney would indicate symptoms of severe and violent repression on principle–where the entire emotional life had been so subjected to continuous frustration because of an ethical standard that the outraged eros reacted upon the body either with acute nephritis or it may be with cancer.

Where there is trouble with the legs, the patient being unable to stand and confined to the bed, some psychological thinkers proffer some such explanation as this. The legs are the things we stand on, that which gives support to the body. In the symbolic pageantry utilised by the Unconscious–and it must be understood that the activity of the Unconscious proceeds almost exclusively through what are to us symbols–the instinctual life is our mental support. It is that which we tend to rely upon, our stability and foundation, during life. Should therefore our understanding of life fall short of what it should be for us–and obviously that standard varies with different people–so that we unduly repress our instincts to the point when the resulting sense of insecurity and anxiety become intolerable, the psyche achieves a revenge through an affliction of the supports of the personality. Thus it is that we learn, so it is said, by illness. When our supports, no matter of what nature, have been annihilated, we sometimes seek to enquire into causes and origins. When the enquiry is honestly furthered, with a sincere view to self-knowledge, and internal resistance broken down by meditation or analysis, no doubt recovery would ensue. That is to say, the disappearance of alarming symptoms, and a return of normal function.

The solvent to these difficulties, the practical solution of the problem, consists primarily in the elimination so far as possible of fear. Of course, from the larger point of view, fear is an essential part of our make-up. Man is so puny a creature on the face of the earth, and Nature is vast and terrible in her operations. How else could it be that fear eats at the heart of each of us? But this is a wholesome fear–fear of the future, fear of position, a needless worrying about affairs which cannot be helped or changed, at least not by hugging a constant fear that they will change in a manner that is painful and sad. From the spiritual point of view, fears such as we have named act as a great freezer, as an inhibitor of action and the free flow of vital energy from within. The man who is afraid to embark upon a given course of action because it may lead to failure, or whose apprehension of success and of the future generally, is hardly likely to accomplish very much. "Fear is failure" says one magical aphorism, "and the forerunner of failure. Be thou therefore without fear, for in the heart of the coward, virtue abideth not."

One of the most interesting instances of the psycho-therapeutic attitude to fear and anxiety and the escape-problem as a whole was Groddeck's treatment, when he was a physician before applying psychology to his problems, of certain cases of indigestion and nervous dyspepsia. One of the psychological theorems regarding this form of discomfort is that it is due to anxiety. We all know how bad news or worry affects the digestion, from turning the food sour to taking away the appetite. But the root cause of this particular anxiety is not the problem in hand, but the anxiety which has its roots in an early conflict and is made the worse by the occurrence of an immediate problem evoking conflict and anxiety. Groddeck's treatment–almost the homeopathic principle–emphasised or comprised a diet of precisely those foods which formerly disagreed with his patient. If eggs were the cause of indigestion the diet would comprise eggs until eventually the psychic would give up attempting to evade the associations which had been linked to eggs, and the digestive trouble would in time disappear. To force the psyche to face its problems and accept them was his idea rather than that the psyche should continually balk from and attempt to flee the symptoms it threw up in the body. The unconditional acceptance of the conflict, and the associations connected with it, was the first step towards cure. The technique is, in a word or two, an attack on the escape mechanism. Integrity cannot be won by an escapist attitude towards life. The reward of the attitude which escapes from problems and the reality of life is more likely than not to be nothing but the gnawing pain of guilt and sin.

The same method is often made use of in other forms of therapy. Amongst these, for example, is the treatment of nightmares by analysis. The terror experienced in nightmare, causing the dreamer to awaken bathed in perspiration, angered by a palpitation of the heart, and experiencing an inexplicable sense of impending catastrophe, is likewise due to some conflict or other. Its nature, being unconscious, can only be determined by the context of the dream, and by the lengthy process of confession, free association, and reductive analysis.

But if the dreamer can be trained in his waking state to realise that the nightmare is only the expression of an internal conflict, then he has proceeded halfway to the point where it will cease to bother him. He must accept the presence of such a disorder rather than attempt to escape it, because escape is not an adequate solution of a psychic problem.

This discovery was brought home to us during the war. Amongst the soldiers at the front were those who would not recognise the very obvious fact, that war was a dangerous matter and that they were afraid. This they would not accept, though underneath a veritable torrent of fear was raging, and the whole of the instinctive impulse was to bolt from the scene of battle. Those who recognised this impulse but at the same time saw that flight was impossible and that the war had to be seen through, came to no mental or spiritual harm. It was the former type, suffering from a terrible fear but boasting that they were not in the least afraid, who become affected by shell-shock. Shell-shock–the shock experienced by the nervous system through the devastating noise of explosion, had nothing to do with their actual trouble at all. The cause was simply a cowardly refusal to face the conflict raging in the psyche. And when this became so intolerable, an actual split occurred in consciousness, so that there was a gap in memory, awareness and in efficiency.

With the acceptance of the theory of conflict as a cause of nightmare, a subtle change gradually creeps into the nightmare-dream. The following is one rather fine example, together with the method of dealing with it.

A woman patient frequently dreamed that she was hanging from a rope in a room which had an enormously high ceiling, about fifty or sixty feet high. The rope was affixed by a hook to the ceiling, and the weight imposed upon the hook was gradually loosening the plaster around. Any moment, the hook would tear loose from the ceiling, and the body would be dashed to the ground. At this juncture of the dream, unable to face the terror of being hurled to death on the ground, the woman awoke in a frenzy of fear, screaming. The advice given in this particular case–and since the dream is a typical nightmare, the same technique may be widely recommended–was to suggest to the woman the advisability of meditating on the dream before falling to sleep at night. The suggestion was to lengthen the term of the dream so as to invite the nightmare and observe what happened when the plaster did finally break, tearing the hook from the ceiling.

Constant and deep reflection on the dream's theme before sleep was the method by which the Unconscious could so be influenced as to induce a vigilant attitude even during the progress of phantasy. The topic of meditation would also be the conscious application of the idea of non-resistance. Let the catastrophe occur, and see what happens. If the phantasy is being perched on a high cliff and at any moment there is the danger of being hurled to the ground, awaking at mid-point in a sweat of fear, then gradually train the mind to thrust out all resistance to the fall. By methods such as these resistance is eliminated from the sphere of consciousness.

Here, some word should be said about repression and the means of its elimination. A great many people have come to believe, through a very casual reading of some of the early psycho-analytic literature, that psychology countenances the removal of repression by means which are unethical and anti-social. Nothing could be further from the truth. Repression is always defined as an unconscious and automatic process. It is a process by which the personality protects itself against distasteful concepts, by thrusting them without the horizon of consciousness into the dark and forbidding region of the Unconscious. Since this process begins very early in life, the Unconscious is by middle age stuffed with a mass of repressed material—ideas about parents and relatives, associations connected with environment, infantile beliefs and actions. Suppression, on the other hand, is a deliberate and conscious thing. It presupposes a process on conscious selection and elimination, in which one alternative is suppressed in favour of another.

It is repression, the unconscious process of thrusting things out of sight, which is the dangerous method. It is dangerous because repressed emotions and feelings lock up memory and power in the Unconscious. Because ideas become associated with each other, forming definite complexes, there is, if repressed memories begin to grow by association, a splitting off of one side of the mind at the expense of the other with a consequent locking up of energy and vitality which should be available for the entire personality. The conquest of repression proceeds as with the conquest of internal conflict previously described.

There is no need to live an anti-social or vicious life, one of self-indulgence or of degradation as so many people think. To be free from a repression does not argue that one should have behaved like "a young man about town." Though that is not to say that a reasonable satistfaction of the instinctual life should be eschewed where this is at all possible. But the frank realisation and acceptance of the human personality as many-sided, and a refusal to blind oneself to experience no matter of what kind, will go far towards relieving the partition erected between the Unconscious and the Conscious, and removing resistance and repression.

To restate the attitude expounded in this chapter, I conceive of analytical psychology as the spouse of the ancient system of Magic. For psychology has succeeded in evolving a system which can be applied to almost any individual who wishes to know the several departments and constituents of his own personality. Possibly for the first time in the history of civilised thought, there is a technique which is of inestimable value to the average man. It is of supreme value to the student of Magic and Mysticism, who, too often, labours under several delusions of what it is that he hopes to accomplish, and in what length of time he will do so. A study of analysis will prove first of all that he cannot proceed quicker than his own Unconscious permits him. This will prevent gate-crashing, and an irrational enthusiasm and desire for speed. Secondly, through the elimination of erroneous ideas as to himself, the phantasms of wish-fulfilment and insensate day-dreaming, he will have obtained a more comprehensive account of what magical and meditation systems can accomplish, and what degree of achievement in these spheres is open to him. He will be entirely less subject to delusion and deception because his attraction to Magic will not have been caused by the unconscious desire to escape from the pressing problems of his immediate existence with which he finds himself unable efficiently to cope.

Moreover, he will have familiarised himself with the true extent of his own sense of inferiority. The compulsive necessity of becoming unduly aggressive because of an imagined or pathological inferiority will not longer urge him to an intolerable sense of deficiency. Being acquainted with the fundamental problem of insecurity which every thinking individual is bound to have, since man is so apparently insignificant and unimportant when compared to the vastness of the universe, he will not be liable to adopt extreme religious or scientific notions from so-called spiritual experience or laboratory experiment to buttress up his own desire for some one thing which is secure and reliable.

Analysis is the logical precursor of spiritual attainment and magical experiment. It should comprise definitely the first stage of spiritual training. Were it possible, and were there magical schools in existence, it would gratify me enormously to see magical training preceded by six or twelve months of application to reductive analysis, pursued by sympathetic physicians or lay-analysts who had long and intimate experience with clinical work. The magical schools must open a Department of Analytical Psychology, if their own systems are to attain public prominence worthy of attention and patronage. Such schools, though offering courses of training considerably prolonged, would eventually develop such a type of individual that the public would eliminate "dangerous" from its association with Magic, and be obliged to take cognisance of the soundness of its technique. This union of two systems would, for Magic at any rate, build up psychological credit, and a sense of great reliability and prestige would accrue to it.

One of the greatest obstacles to success in Magic, to any kind of worth-while result in the mystical sciences, is that the psycho-emotional system of its average student is hopelessly clogged with infantile and adolescent predilections which have not been recognised as such. The ego is compelled to extreme courses of action, as though by compulsion. And underneath his every activity lurks the unconscious spectre–fear. It is precisely with these monsters of phantasy that analytical psychology can deal effectively, and it is from such absurd obstacles that the magical student is a confirmed but unconscious sufferer.

By associating Magic with analysis, we should be able to avoid the pitfalls into which our predecessors fell so headlong. The production of genius–more specifically a religious and mystical type of genius–ever the goal of Magic, should be more within our grasp than ever before, and considerably more open to achievement.

These ideas are mentioned not because a systematic union of Magic and Psychology will be here presented, but in the hope that this effort will spur some psychologist acquainted with magical and mystical techniques to attempt such a task. Whoever does succeed in welding the two indissolubly together, to him mankind will ever be grateful. For such a union comprises the marriage of the archaic with the modern, the Unconscious with the Conscious–the precursor of the birth of the Golden Flower not for any individual alone but for mankind as a whole.

THE INNER GUIDE MEDITATION
A Spiritual Technology for the 21st Century
By Edwin C. Steinbrecher
Foreword by Israel Regardie

The investigation of the inner world of the soul has long been the special province of what is known as occultism. Some forms of religion have also attempted much the same task–especially the Eastern ones–limited, however, by some original revelation which hampered the free reign of scientific method. It is only in relatively recent times that some schools of modern psychology have turned their attention to that same area, and in the process of doing so developed their own peculiar techniques. The latter, curiously enough, bear many resemblances to the more archaic methods that are referred to as occult.

The author of this little handbook on meditation deserves an enormous amount of credit for first having approached the possibility of such methods through the medium of analytical psychology, the method of Carl G. Jung. Since Steinbrecher was an astrologer years before becoming an analyst and, it did not take him long to perceive relationships and thus to attempt some kind of unification of these different sets of ideas and techniques. So his handbook describes an amalgam of Jung's use of creative imagination, astrology and the tarot. The author evidently knows what he is doing, for he has evolved a viable system of self-discovery with all sorts of fascinating overtones and undertones. The book is clearly written, the technique vividly and plainly described so that there is little room for misunderstanding as to what the author means. The meditations often yield up entirely new and unexpected types of information and interpretation relative to the meaning of the tarot, for example, and their relation to the planetary symbols–and in turn to the psycho-physical structure of the student.

Steinbrecher's directions are unambiguous and should be intelligible to anybody with the least capacity for imaginative or occult work. I am certain this book, from the very tentative first edition of only a few years ago to the umpteenth yet to come, will go down in occult history as one of the most significant contributions to meditation in modern times. Edwin Steinbrecher deserves any praise and commendation that is handed out to him, for he has labored long and patiently in this field especially to make *The Inner Guide Meditation* the classic that it is well on its way to becoming.

Israel Regardie

Sedona, Arizona
1983

THE TEACHERS OF FULFILLMENT
Foreword by Israel Regardie
New Falcon Publishing, Third Revised Edition, 2017

This book is a presentation in brief of the major metaphysical systems now operative here and throughout the world. Amongst its other aims was to demonstrate how these various systems have evolved from the stem and root of Mary Baker Eddy's Christian Science. This is why so much space has been given to a consideration of her personality, her life and work.

One of my friends of many years ago, the late Dr. Hereward Carrington complained that I was leaning over backwards in my attempt to be fair to Mrs. Eddy. If this is in fact the case, then I must confess to a profound respect for this really extraordinary woman. Insofar as she was constantly ill and a self-confessed failure through to her sixtieth year, it seems a remarkable achievement to have completely turned around the direction of her spiritual energies for creative ends during the remaining years of her life. There are not many people of whom this can be said. The average person is fairly well played out by sixty. The fires of life are beginning to dim, if not to go out altogether. She is thus worthy of detailed study and attention.

What she also had to say is no less significant. Perhaps she might not agree with an ancient injunction to "enflame thyself with prayer," but nonetheless whatever success Christian Scientists have had with their "demonstrations" must surely depend on an enormous amount of intensity and concentration. This may not be immediately evoked, but given sufficient time and study and prayer I am certain this inner enthusiasm must arise. And this is the *sine qua non* of success.

It reminds me of some of the stories told by Emily Cady of the Unity School of Christianity. It is said she used to pace up and down her study, concentrating utterly on her affirmations and denials, and the contents of her prayers. In this way, she achieved the fulfillment of her desires through enflaming her mind in prayer. Her intensity was the dynamic factor which bought about the results in various fields of life activities for which she is known.

There are almost exact parallels to these examples in many widely disparate areas. The gulf between them is so wide the individual protagonists within those fields would very likely be horrified to see this parallelism drawn.

For example in the book *Sacred Magic of Abremelin the Mage* translated by the renowned occult scholar of the past century S. Liddell Mathers there is a description of a process of enlightenment which entails total withdrawal from the world for a period of six full months, beginning at Easter in any given year. The whole time cycle is to be spent praying to the Almighty that he vouchsafe illumination to the student and help him obtain the Knowledge and Conversation of his Holy Guardian Angel. Prayers are more or less scattered at the outset of the retreat. There are many tasks to be performed. But as the time proceeds, more or less all the hours of the day and night come to be spent in fervent and ardent prayer. This is the book where is first found the phrase "enflame thyself in prayer."

Now compare this with the experience of one of the founders of the modern Pentecostal movement. It is described at some length in *They Speak With Other Tongues* by J. L. Sherrill (Spire Books, Old Tapper, N.J., 1973) A young Methodist minister Charles F. Parham decided he must do something about his religious life. He had found it wanting when compared with the experiences described in the New Testament. So, in the year 1900, he set out in Topeka, Kansas, to see whether he could discover the secret of living faith which was so conspicuous by it absence in his heart. He was reasonably sure it existed; the scriptures were adamant on that score. "The next morning, everyone in Stone's Folly joined in this prayer. They prayed throughout the morning and into the afternoon. The atmosphere around the mansion was charged with expectancy. But the sun went down and nothing unusual had occurred.

"Then about seven o'clock that night–it was New Year's Eve, 1900–a young student named Agnes N. Ozman remembered something. Wasn't it true that many of the Baptisms described in Acts were accompanied by an action, as well as prayer? Miss Ozman went to find Charles Parham. She told him about her thought.

'Would you pray for me in this way?' she asked.

Parham hesitated just long enough to utter a short prayer about the righteousness of what they were doing. Then, gently he placed his two hands on Miss Ozman's head. Immediately, quietly, there came from her lips a flow of syllables neither one of them could understand.

At Stone's Folly, everyone now prayed with increased fervor for the coming of the Holy Spirit. Over the next three days there were many Baptisms, each one signaled by the mysterious tongues. On January 3, Parham himself and a dozen other ministers from various denominations present with him in this room received the Baptism and spoke in tongues."

It is this fervor which in no way differs from the prayer based on the scriptures and Science and Health which apparently is the indispensable factor leading to success, though I am sure each particular group could cite dozens of different reasons to emphasize the vast differences between them. In the last resort, however, these are of little account.

Another example of this from an entirely different quarter comes from Aleister Crowley. He was no stranger to these phenomena, however incredulous one may be. After all, he was the modern writer who to a great extent has popularized the phrase "Enflame thyself in prayer." In his early thirties, shortly after his return from a visit to the lower borders of China, he wrote a series of what came to be called the Holy Books. Highly inspirational, he considered them in a totally different category from all his other literary work. In one of the *Liber VII vel Lapidis Lazuli*, there is an opening section entitled "Prologue of the Unborn." And it is here that the evidence presents itself that he was once in the company, as it were, of the Pentecostalists and present day charismatic adherents. "To me only the distant flute, the abiding vision of Pan. On all sides Pan to the eye, to the ear: The perfume of Pan pervading, the taste of him utterly filling my mouth, so that the tongue breaks forth into a weird and monstrous speech."

Is this so far from Pentecostalism and the Baptism by the Holy Spirit?

Though this does not deal per se with the technique or methods employed by the various metaphysical movements, enough actually is stated to enable the interested student to formulate his own technique. There is so little difference, ultimately, between any of them, that this should present no real problem. It is only when metaphysics is left behind and the area of the occult and practical magic is approached that there appears a vast gulf. This however in no wise concerns us here and now, though even in this area, the Abramelin injunction still holds good.

The intensity can be of a quiet apparently restrained type so typical for example, of the Episcopal Church or the Christian Scientist, or it could be of the more overt emotion of the Pentecostalist or, let us say, of the Bhakti yogi of the Indian continent. Without this, there is nothing. And nothing can not persuade the window of heaven to open to scatter its largess on the petitioner.

I had intended many year ago to include a chapter on the work of the late Ernest Holmes. For one of several reasons the task eluded me until one Saturday morning some years ago I ran into him in a flower shop on La Brea Boulevard just north of Wilshire

Boulevard in Los Angeles. Having heard him speak many times a the Wilshire Ebell Theatre where he held his services on Sunday mornings I recognized him immediately. Having introduced myself we had a very pleasant chat; he was very friendly and open. This moved me, at least in determination, to write a chapter about him, his life long quest and his very successful work in some subsequent edition of this book. But the exigencies of everyday life and the pressure relative to the maintenance of a psychological practice proved too much to permit me to devote any thought or time to writing this very necessary essay.

Now that I have retired to the quiet mountains of Arizona I am still a little undecided as to how to approach this essay on Holmes. He is a considerably different person from most of the people mentioned in this book. For while he is indebted to some extent to Mrs. Eddy, many other thinkers and philosophers have had a broadening effect on his metaphysical approach which demands a bit more attention to the development of his inner life than was necessary with the others. I felt therefore more time was needed for me to absorb the spirit of his metaphysical contribution. This is taking a great deal more time and effort and contemplation than I originally anticipated, and so to date this essay remains only in rudimentary form in my mind. I would fancy that in the very near future some clarification may develop about this very solid and enthusiastic teacher which will permit finally the completion of my evaluation of both him as a person and Science of Mind as a system. When that day arrives, whenever that will be, I am sure my publishers will include it in this volume or another.

Israel Regardie

Arizona
1983

New Falcon Publications
**Publisher of Controversial Books and CDs
Invites You to Visit Our Website:
http://www.newfalcon.com**

At the Falcon website you can:

- Browse the online catalog of all our great titles, including books by Robert Anton Wilson, Christopher S. Hyatt, Israel Regardie, Aleister Crowley, Timothy Leary, Osho, Lon Milo DuQuette and many more
- Find out what's available and what's out of stock
- Get special discounts
- Order our titles through our secure online server
- Find products not available anywhere else including:
    - One of a kind and limited availability products
    - Special packages
    - Special pricing
- And much, much more

Get online today at http://www.newfalcon.com